Catalog

No. 31

VISALIA STOCK SADDLE Co.

COPYRIGHT, 1938

SAN FRANCISCO, CAL.

2117 - 2123

MARKET ST.

Original catalog (1938) front cover.

Saddle and Western Gear Catalog, 1938

Visalia Stock Saddle Co.

Introduction and Bibliography by
Victor M. Linoff

DOVER PUBLICATIONS, INC.
Mineola, New York

Published in Canada by General Publishing Company, Ltd., 30 Lesmill Road, Don Mills, Toronto, Ontario.

Bibliographical Note

This Dover edition, first published in 1999, is an unabridged republication of the *Visalia Stock Saddle Co. Catalog No. 31,* originally published 1938, San Francisco. A new Introduction and Bibliography have been specially prepared by Victor M. Linoff for this edition.

Library of Congress Cataloging-in-Publication Data

Visalia Stock Saddle Co. catalog no. 31
    Saddle and western gear catalog, 1938 / Visalia Stock Saddle Co.; Victor M. Linoff, editor.
        p.   cm.
    Originally published: Visalia Stock Saddle Co. catalog no. 31. San Francisco : Visalia Stock Saddle Co., 1938, with new introd. and bibliography.
    Includes bibliographical references.
    ISBN 0-486-40720-9 (pbk.)
    1. Visalia Stock Saddle Co. Catalogs. 2. Western saddles—California Catalogs. 3. Western riding—Equipment and supplies Catalogs. I. Linoff, Victor M. II. Visalia Stock Saddle Co. III. Title.
TS1033.V574   1999
685'.1'0294—dc21   99-35140
                                              CIP

Manufactured in the United States of America
Dover Publications, Inc., 31 East 2nd Street, Mineola, N.Y. 11501

INTRODUCTION

Victor M. Linoff

THE COWBOY . . . FROM FRONTIER TO FILM

The 1930's were a turbulent time in America. The carefree character of the twenties had given way to the harsh reality of the Great Depression and World War II loomed on the horizon. Escapism was a popular survival strategy and with the addition of sound, motion pictures began presenting the most potent form of escapism available to Americans.

It is easy to imagine that larger-than-life heroes, like the cowboy, would emerge under these circumstances. The Depression and Hollywood both helped shape a new image for the cowboy. It was the age of Tom Mix, Hoot Gibson, Tim McCoy, Ken Maynard, and John Wayne. In 1934 a young Gene Autry introduced a new kind of western character: the singing cowboy. The following year marked the debut of Hopalong Cassidy and Roy Rogers, who, with his handsome palomino Trigger, soon earned the appellation "The King of the Cowboys."

Meanwhile, on radio, the world first had heard the exploits of the Lone Ranger at the height of the Depression in 1930. The program's theme music, Rossini's *William Tell* Overture, may have been one of the first successful crossovers of classical music into the popular market.

Hollywood contributed significantly towards the creation of a truly unique American icon. In the 1930's alone more than 1000 Westerns were produced. These provided audiences with an idyllic image of the freedom of the frontier. Americans fell in love with the "romance" of the cowboy and life on the open range. There was just one problem: The representation was entirely a contrivance of Hollywood's fertile imagination. Westerns failed to accurately portray the drudgery and solitude that were characteristic of the real cowboy's life.

In addition, real, working cowboys, like so many Americans, were in transition. The Western frontier was rapidly shrinking and the cowboy's old routines were being supplanted by technology. Horses were slowly giving way to the greater horsepower and speed of trucks, and other machines. In effect, Americans and their film industry were in love with a hero and a way of life that was vanishing.

Over time, disappearing range life was translated into a unique, stylized series of popular competitions collectively called the American Rodeo. The prowess and diverse skills that had once pitted a cowboy in a daily life-and-death contest against nature and beast could still be displayed in the rodeo arena.

It is within this context that the Visalia Stock Saddle Company published its Catalog No. 31, offering a panoply of goods for the working, "wannabe," and Hollywood cowboy.

THE VISALIA STOCK SADDLE COMPANY

Until the opening of the transcontinental railroad in 1869, California was extremely remote and isolated. Consequently, the culture of its first Mexican and Spanish settlers was the major influence on its manufacturing and crafts. That is why the California saddle evolved into something quite different from the English-influenced Eastern or the more rugged Texas saddles. Generally, California saddles were lighter in weight, and often more elaborately carved and ornamented.

Because of its temperate climes and ample, fertile grazing land, the broad San Joaquin Valley, where Visalia is located, attracted most of the Spanish cattle ranchers settling in California. By 1850, Visalia was a burgeoning cow town. Ideally situated on the main mail route about halfway between Los Angeles and San Francisco, Visalia, at its peak, boasted nearly ten prestigious saddlemaking firms and was recognized for producing some of the finest saddles in the state.

Saddlemaker Juan Martarel (d. 1894) was third to open shop in Visalia. Born and trained in San Salvador, Martarel first took his craft to Hornitas (present-day Hornitos), Mariposa County, California in the late 1850's. In 1868 he relocated his business to the more bustling Visalia. Two skilled, long-time employees moved with him.

Ricardo Mattlé, a saddlemaker from Sonora, Mexico began working for Martarel in 1860. Mattlé is credited with being a major influence in the transformation of the traditional Vaquero saddle into something uniquely American. Another Martarel artisan, Alsalio Herrea, was a talented bit and spur maker noted for his silver mountings.

But Martarel was apparently a better craftsman than businessman. By 1870, competition had put him in financial trouble and he considered closing. At the eleventh hour, two Englishmen—Walker and Shuhman—saved the day by purchasing Martarel's enterprise.

David E. Walker (d. 1894) and Henry Gust Shuhman (b. 1842) met and became friends in London, Ontario. Like many others, they saw an opportunity to strike it rich in California. By 1865 they were in San Francisco gaining invaluable saddlemaking experience at the prestigious Main & Winchester Saddlery. Established in 1849 by Charley Main and E. H. Winchester, this firm was one of California's earliest, largest, and best saddleries. Walker and Shuhman eventually became so skilled that they were given the assignment to produce a set of double harness for President Ulysses S. Grant. This recognition gave them the incentive to strike out on their own. As Visalia was becoming the leading commerce center for the San Joaquin Valley, they believed it would provide the perfect locale for their new enterprise.

By early 1870 Walker and Shuhman were ensconced at 60 Main Street. Faced with the competition of two established saddlemakers they were delighted by the opportunity to buy out Martarel. As a condition of purchase, Walker & Shuhman retained the valuable skills of Martarel and his employees. Soon after, they hired José Rodriguez, a most capable saddlemaker from Bakersfield who possessed special expertise in the design of the "tree"—the heart of the saddle. Thus, the Visalia Stock Saddle Company was born. It grew rapidly and prospered, and soon the *D. E. Walker* brand on saddles was the standard for cowboys all along the West Coast.

The Walker–Shuhman partnership endured just until 1877. Differences in business philosophy were the primary cause of the break-up. Shuhman bought out the interests of his partner, retaining the employees and rights to the Visalia Stock Saddle Co. name. Both remained in Visalia, operating independent, competing enterprises. Walker, the more aggressive advertiser and marketer, continued producing and energetically promoting saddlery under his original *D. E. Walker* brand name.

In 1879, Shuhman sold the Visalia business back to Walker who then operated it on his own until 1887. That same year a Mr. Wade, who had been the general manager of another prominent San Francisco manufactory, F. S. Johnson and Company, became Walker's partner. The new alliance brought the Visalia Stock Saddle Company greater exposure and an entrance into the larger and more lucrative San Francisco market. The partnership's San Francisco-made saddles bore a *Wade & Walker* imprint, however Walker remained sole owner of his Visalia business, preserving the *D. E. Walker* stamp for his exclusive use. The company underwent further change in 1892 when Wade's interest was purchased by Henry Wegener. Thereafter, saddles were branded *Walker & Wegener.*

Shortly before his death in 1894, Walker closed the Visalia operation to concentrate on the expanding San Francisco enterprise. He also brought Edmund Walker Weeks, his talented nephew from Canada, into the company. With the passing of Henry Wegener in about 1899, Weeks, who had inherited his uncle's interests, bought the former partner's shares in the business from Wegener's widow. As sole owner Weeks now possessed the ability to reshape the dynamic Visalia Company and to position it for the challenges of the upcoming twentieth century.

Weeks undertook an ambitious expansion program. He added employees and increased his catalog advertising. In 1900 he moved the business, for the third time since it had settled in San Francisco, to new and larger quarters at 510 Market Street. The 1906 Earthquake destroyed that site, forcing a final relocation to 2117-2123 Market Street, where the company remained for nearly half a century.

Returning to the use of the powerful and long-recognized *D. E. Walker* brand name, Weeks continued driving the Visalia Stock Saddle Company forward right up until his own death in the early 1930's. Catalog No. 31 was issued after Weeks' passing, but it credits Walker as "the founder" and Weeks as "the builder" of the company.

After Weeks' death, his grandson, the less talented Leland Bergen, ran the business into decline until finally selling it to Sheldon Potter in 1945. However, Potter, who had grown up in the cattle business, possessed the acumen to return the Visalia Company to its original luster. Potter also moved the company into expanded quarters in Sacramento, since by the early 1950's San Francisco was no longer the right place for a saddlemaking firm.

In June of 1958 Kenneth R. Coppock acquired the venerable old concern. Coppock was a successful Calgary, Canada saddlemaker who had founded the Canadian Kenway Saddle and Leather Company, a firm that grew to be the largest in Canada. The merging of the two companies made for a powerful international empire. (The capable Potter stayed on to manage the Sacramento affairs.) But when a disastrous fire virtually destroyed the Sacramento factory in the early sixties, Coppock retreated to his Canadian interests. The Visalia name, goodwill, and what remained of any manufacturing equipment were purchased by several dedicated, long-standing employees. They reestablished operations in Castro Valley, California.

Because of the many innovations introduced over nine decades by the Visalia Company, it is now accepted as California's most important and influential saddlemaker.

THE KYNE CONNECTION

Even in the midst of the Depression, the Visalia Stock Saddle Company was a dominant force in its industry, and the glowing celebrity endorsement in the foreword to Catalog No. 31 is evidence of this.

The author of this foreword, Peter Bernard Kyne (1880–1957), was a popular, prolific writer. From the teens through World War II, he authored more than a thousand short stories for such periodicals as *American, Cosmopolitan, Colliers, Saturday Evening Post* and *Sunset* magazines. He also wrote twenty-five heroic novels ranging from Westerns to sea stories, military tales, and inspirational fiction. Between 1921 and 1952 nearly two dozen of his stories, like "Three Godfathers" and "Pride of Palomar," were made into motion pictures. Kyne is credited with having been an influential contributor to the shaping of the Hollywood Western genre.

Born in San Francisco to a father in the cattle ranching business, Kyne's youth must have provided the inspiration for his Western writings. The adventures of his young adulthood must have helped furnish the fodder for his other, non-Western, fiction: At sixteen he left home to become a clerk in the general store of a nearby town. Nine months later, lying about his age, he enlisted in the army. After a year of service in the Philippines he returned to San Francisco to work as a salesman for a variety of businesses, including a wholesale lumber firm. Eventually, he opened his own haberdashery.

Kyne's first short story "A Little Matter of Salvage" appeared in the *Saturday Evening Post* in 1909. Twenty-five years later, when the catalog was published, Kyne's career was waning, the stereotypical style of his writing having gradually lost public favor. Ill health was also making work difficult for him. There is no doubt, though, that Kyne's endorsement contributed significantly to the marketing strength of Catalog No. 31. Through his connection with the film industry, it is likely that Kyne was also able to help boost sales to that important market segment.

As a long-time, prominent resident of San Francisco, it is very likely that Kyne was personally acquainted with Edmund Walker Weeks and may have written the foreword to Catalog No. 31 as a favor. Whether or not he received compensation is a matter of conjecture.

THE CATALOG

David Walker first marketed his products via direct mail and handbills. He soon began producing catalogs that allowed remote customers to view and purchase his goods without ever visiting his shop.

While Catalog No. 31 carries a cover copyright of 1938, there are indications that it may have been distributed at least three years prior. Clearly, it circulated many times longer than today's catalogs do. During the 1930's goods were still produced without planned obsolescence—a successful product enjoyed a long life. The styles of western tack, clothing and accessories changed little from year to year or decade to decade for that matter. Prices might change, and indeed Catalog No. 31 was reissued with revised pricing, but the products were marketed for many years.

Catalog No. 31 is remarkable for the depth of the merchandise it offered. The index lists nearly 120 different items: everything from Bickmore's Gall Cure to Ding skirts and angora chaps. For those who desired only a representation of cowboy life, Visalia tantalized its readers with a set of twelve Charles M. Russell pictures for $2.50 (p. 124). One dollar would buy "The Jo Mora Cowboy and Rodeo Map" (p. 122) or a set of six sketches by Lee M.

Rice (pp. 126–127). (Rice [1892–1984] was primarily an accomplished saddlemaker, but was also noted for his drawings, research, and writings on the West. In 1975 he co-authored *They Saddled the West,* a fundamental text that contains a full chapter on the history of the Visalia Company.)

Much of Catalog No. 31's special character derives from its quaint cowboy language, dry humor and incidental illustrations of Western life. What better way to describe the quality of their saddles than by proclaiming: "Walker's—The Saddle You 'Swear By'—But Not At" or "Send in your old stuff and let us surprise you—If we can't repair it, it can't be repaired."

Naturally a substantial portion of the catalog is devoted to the renowned saddles and accessories produced by Visalia. They took their work seriously; so much so that two pages are devoted to elaborate "directions for ordering saddles" (pp. 46–47). Their own goods are supplemented by those of other prominent manufacturers—H. J. Justin & Sons boots, Starnes boots, John B. Stetson hats, Levi Strauss and Lee cowboy overalls.

For those who could afford it, the ultimate "cowboy" escape could be had at one of the Western dude ranches that began proliferating in the '30's. Visalia made sure that they were addressing that up-and-coming market with inexpensive tack and supplies.

It is impressive that even during the Depression, Visalia possessed sufficient confidence in their products to be offering high-end silver mounted saddles for as much as $350.00. Although some saddles were priced under $75.00, it is important to consider that at this time many Americans were subsisting on less than five dollars a week!

Within the pages of this catalog is a wealth of information for researchers and historians. From the impressive product illustrations and detailed descriptions to helpful hints and veterinary advice, Catalog No. 31 represents the apotheosis of Western life in the 1930's, and testifies to the long-term dominance of the Visalia Company. It also enables those of us still smitten with the "romance" of cowboy lore to climb up into the saddle and "return to those thrilling days of yesteryear" when the cowboy ruled the range. As Peter Kyne encourages: "NOW READ THE CATALOG" and enjoy!

ACKNOWLEDGMENTS
AND BIBLIOGRAPHY

A very special thank-you to Wendy Inman for her invaluable assistance in researching this history. Thanks, also, to the following for their valued service: the City of Mesa (Arizona) Public Library reference staff, who guided me to important resources; and Rosalie Longan and Anna Marie Zimmerman of the Tulare (California) Public Library, who provided important material.

BOOKS
Buscombe, Edward, ed. *The BFI Companion to the Western.* New York: Da Capo Press, Inc., 1988.

Chamberlain, Dick and Jeff Edwards. *Saddles and Saddle Makers of Porterville.* Privately printed, 1982.

Hutchins, Dan and Sebi. *Old Cowboy Saddles and Spurs: Identifying the Craftsmen Who Made Them, Fourth Annual.* Santa Fe, NM: Horse Feathers Publishing Co., nd.

Mackin, Bill. *Cowboy and Gunfighter Collectibles.* Missoula, MT: Mountain Press Publishing Company, 1995.

Manns, William and Elizabeth Clair Flood. *Cowboys and the Trappings of the Old West.* Santa Fe, NM: Zon International Publishing Company, 1997.

McCutcheon, Marc. *The Writer's Guide to Everyday Life from Prohibition through World War II.* Cincinnati, OH: Writer's Digest Books, 1995.

Nottage, James H. *Saddlemaker to the Stars: The Leather and Silver Art of Edward Bohlin.* Los Angeles, CA: Autry Museum of Western Heritage, 1996.

Rice, Lee M. and Glenn R. Vernam. *They Saddled the West.* Cambridge, MD: Cornell Maritime Press, Inc., 1975.

Smith, James F., Jr. "Peter B. Kyne." *Dictionary of Literary Biography, Vol. 78: American Short-Story Writers 1880–1910.* Detroit MI: Gale Research, Inc. 1989.

PERIODICALS

Los Tulares: Quarterly Bulletin of the Tulare County Historical Society. Various editions.

FOREWORD

By PETER B. KYNE

In my day I have written forewords to many books, but this is the first time I have ever written a foreword to a catalog. It is a real pleasure, however, to write a foreword to this catalog, for I am familiar with this company's products, having used them all my life.

As a boy eight years old I rode one of the earliest made saddles of D. E. Walker, who established this company in the city of Visalia, California, about sixty-five years ago. My legs were too short to reach the stirrups, even after they had been shortened to the limit, so I used to loop the rosaderos instead. This was a good saddle for two reasons: it suited me, and also one Jose Maria Antonio Sanchez, who, in his youth, had been a great rider in our country, when rough riding was a daily chore and not an exhibition to be paid for.

The design of that old saddle tree remains basically the same to this day, and I have used many of the modern vintage and never with the slightest discomfort or loss of skin to man or beast. In 1928 I took my outfit to the Stampede at Calgary, Alberta, Canada, and was advised by a friendly cowboy to sit in my saddle continuously or some weak brother would steal it. It was interesting to have dozens of the local boys coming up to my hotel room, introducing themselves, and asking to see my saddle. And it wasn't a show saddle, either. Just utilitarian. In the end I lost that saddle. A friend at whose ranch I was a guest raved over its excellences for a week, so I finally gave it to him. He said it had taken me long enough to assimilate the hint.

With the death of D. E. Walker, the Visalia Stock Saddle Company traveled right along in the same old path, under his nephew, Edmund Walker Weeks. Neither the business policy of the firm nor its saddles changed very much. They had a splendid product, it gave universal satisfaction, it was a thing of beauty, so why experiment with changes?

For a trophy, to be contested for in roping contests at rodeos, I am hopelessly addicted to giving a Visalia Stock Saddle, for out in California, cattlemen are suspicious of any other make.

I have bought eight of them thus far, and I use two of them on my own ranch.

After thirty-five years of intimate acquaintance with Visalia saddles, I have never known one to gall a horse's back.

But why confine my commendations to this company's saddles. They sell every article for use in connection with horses and the men and women who ride them, and while I continue to own, ride and race horses I shall always owe them money.

NOW READ THE CATALOG.

Revised Prices Applying to Catalog No. 31

The prices quoted in our catalog No. 31 are several years old, and during this time the cost of most of the materials used in the manufacture of our saddles and other equipment have advanced considerably.

This makes it impossible for us to retail these goods at the prices formerly asked, and still keep our merchandise up to our well-known high standard of quality, and it has become necessary for us to make advances in prices as listed below.

The future is very uncertain as to prices, which are SUBJECT TO CHANGE WITHOUT NOTICE, and which, we hope, will be downward instead of upward, and in which case we will be the first to give our customers the benefit of any fluctuation in costs, without any solicitation on their part.

	Round Skirts	Square Skirts
On all standard weight Saddles, with taps, advance	$3.25	$3.75
On all standard weight Saddles, without taps, advance	2.50	3.00
On Tapaderos, 18 to 23 inch, advance	.50	
On Tapaderos, 24 to 26 inch, advance	.75	

WOOL BLANKETS (page 49)

No. 200—Brown, three fold; present price	$5.75
No. 225—Brown, single; present price	1.95
No. 230—Brown, two fold; present price	4.00
No. 250—Blue, three fold; present price	4.25
No. 275—Blue, two fold; present price	3.00

LEATHER COATS (page 50)

No. 914—Calf skin, present price	$15.00
No. 915—Calf skin, present price	16.00

CHAPS

Armitas, page 58, advance	$1.00
Chaps, shown on pages 59, 60, 61, advance	3.50
Chaps, Nos. 2190, 2180 and 225, page 62, advance	3.00
Chaps, No. 230-X, page 62, advance	2.00
Chaps, Nos. 1402, 1404, 1150, page 63, advance	2.00
Chaps, No. 1175, page 63, advance	1.00
Chaps, Nos. 3100, 3250, 1375, page 64, advance	3.50
Chaps, Nos. 350, 351, 122, 125, page 65, advance	2.50
Chaps, Nos. 160, 150, 140, 130, 135, 165 and 155, page 66, advance	2.50

CHANGES IN JUSTIN BOOT PRICES

No. 615—Present price	$18.00
No. 326-J—Present price	15.00
No. V-563—New Justin Boot, style of 807, but with V tops and three rows stitching, russet color, white piping, sizes from 3 to 11, B width only, rubber heels, Gen calf vamps. A nice light trim boot for	$18.50

CHANGES IN STARNES BOOTS

No. 8305—Present price	$ 7.95
No. 8405—Present price	13.50
No. 1705—Present price	13.50
No. 0355—Present price	15.75
No. 3135—All tan, present price	16.50

BITS (page 97)

No. 719—Present price	$1.65
No. 37—Present price	3.25
No. 39—Present price	2.35
Stewart Electric Clippers, page 126	17.50

CHANGES IN STETSON HAT PRICES

No. 51—Kingston, present price	$11.00
No. 52—Kingway, present price	7.50
No. 25-S—Arminto, present price	9.50
No. 125-S—Austin, present price	9.00
No. 126-S—Austin Chamois	7.50
No. 50-SL—The Visalia Jr.	8.25
No. 5-S—San An Jr.	8.50
No. 5-S—San An, Belly	9.50
No. 15-S—Carlsbad	11.00
No. 31-S—San All	10.50
No. 36-S—Cheunney	12.50
No. 110-S—D. E. Walker	9.00
No. 102-S—San Fran	9.50
No. 106-S—San Fran Jr.	8.50
No. 107-S—San Fran Jr.	8.50
No. 101-SW—San Fran	10.50
No. 32-BS—San Fran, black	9.50
Levi Overalls, page 120	1.95
Levi Jackets, page 120	2.15

NO. 2615—PRICE $9.75
A leader because price makes it so. Vamps full grain black chrome; 11 inches high, single sole, round-toe last, 1¾ inch heel, sizes 5 to 11.

We carry the Non-Slip Horseshoe, with borium caulks, the Cowboy's Malleable Shoes (easily fitted) set of 4..**$2.75**

Send us your subscription for "The Western Horseman" (a bi-monthly magazine for the admirers of the western stock horse). One year **$1.00**

Headstall, No. 908, page 109	$4.50
Headstall, No. 910, page 109	3.25

VISALIA SUPREME QUALITY

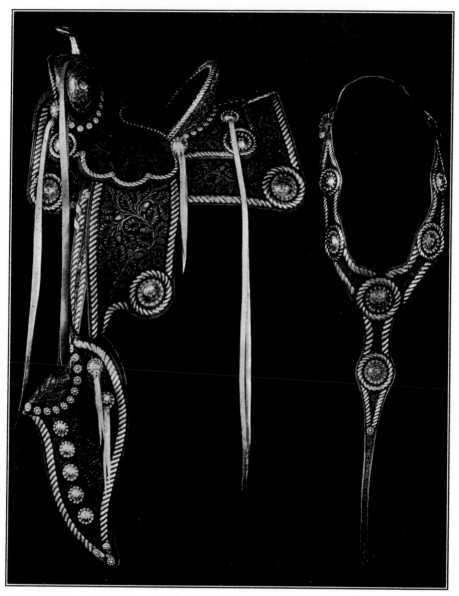

Elegance expressed in refinement and simplicity

THE ROYAL GROUP

The saddles, martingales and bridles shown in the upper corners were made by us for the King and Queen of Serbia and were presented to them as wedding gifts by the Serbians of California.

This saddle shows D. E. WALKER'S artistic designing in silver and leather.

VISALIA QUALITY is to Saddlery
What STERLING QUALITY is to Silver

Yours truly
DAVE E. WALKER

Yours truly
EDM. WALKER WEEKS

STERLING

MARK   QUALITY

(Copyrighted Brands)

For 64 years the name and fame of the Visalia Saddle has been closely associated with the success of the Western cattleman. It is due to the efforts of D. E. Walker, the founder, and of E. W. Weeks, the builder of the Visalia Stock Saddle Company, that Visalia Quality Saddles stand supreme in public regard. Built on the foundation of "A SQUARE DEAL TO ALL," we have consistently maintained the ideal of a good article at as low a price as is consistent with honest material and workmanship

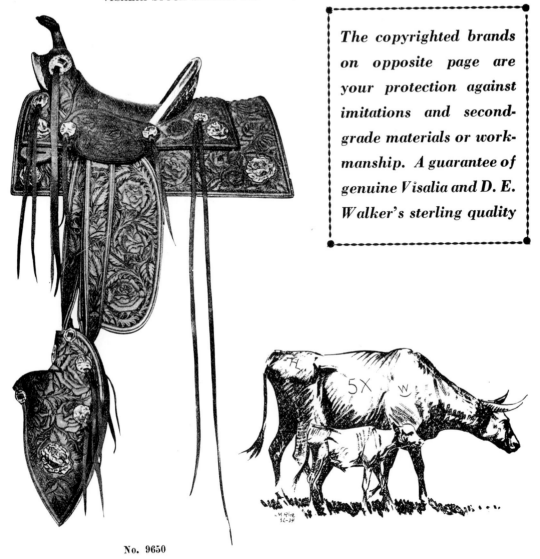

The copyrighted brands on opposite page are your protection against imitations and second-grade materials or workmanship. A guarantee of genuine Visalia and D. E. Walker's sterling quality

No. 9650

FINE ROSE STAMP, with heavy sterling roses, fork and cantle rims, string conchos, shoulder plates and horn cap.

Price as shown.................................$256.60
Without taps 213.50

Less Silver $136.50
Less silver and taps........................... 115.00

Walker Saddles

NONE BETTER - COULD'NT BE

No. 7192   With sterling silver mountings..$300.00
7192-P—No silver... 190.00

A Masterpiece of the saddler's art—as fine a piece of work as you ever saw, probably finer. The size and shape of leathers and tree will be changed to suit your taste. If you are looking for something away out of the ordinary, something that will attract attention any where, you have it here.

Steer heads, true to life; string conchas, name plates, bolt heads, are all heavy sterling silver; solid nickle horn; silver plated solid nickle bound stirrups any size or style.

We Make a Specialty of Extra-Fine Silver-Mounted Saddles, Bridles, Martingales, etc. If interested, write!

"Walker" means Quality

No. 626—As shown $350.00
No. 627—Round skirts 340.00

3¼ inch horn, 5 inch cantle, 14 inch swell fork

WE ALL LIKE ANYTHING CLASSY. To those who can afford it, here is one that will **appeal, for it** has all the sterling qualities that are built into every Walker Saddle, as well as a handsome **appearance,** and will attract attention anywhere, and the price is right. Built on our famous Walker **hand-made tree,** covered with the finest selection of California oak tan leather, and other materials, and **finished** off with high-grade, pure sterling silver trimmings, tastily hand engraved, well-fitted and put on to **stay.** Of course, we make any changes you may want in any part.

Walker Saddles
FOR LONG SERVICE

No. 1625—Price..**$225.00**

Another of our new, exclusive designs, refined, pleasing lines and proportions. A classy job of rose flower stamping, all parts lined and stitched by hand with buckskin. Our famous "Walkeroper" hand-made tree, 3 inch horn, 3½ inch head, 4 inch cantle, slim fork, skirt corners and string conchas of heavy sterling silver, handsomely ornamented with Spanish engravings; ¾ or centre fire, fine hand-made mane or mohair cinch any width; any changes made in tree or leathers to suit the rider. For fine flower stamping the Walker saddles are in a class by themselves.

Walker Saddles
"SOME SADDLES"

No. 1931—ONE OF OUR FINEST...**$275.00**

   We cannot adequately describe the beauty, symmetry and fine lines of this saddle
—the cut shows it better, but still not all that the eyes see. A perfect job of fine
flower stamping with the background blackened, bringing out the floral design in
strong relief. The edges of horn, fork, and cantle, and all leathers are bound with
braided rawhide, giving it a very rich effect as well as a very durable finish. The
string conchas are a new design in heavy sterling silver. We will make any changes
in any part of the saddle to suit your taste.

Walker Saddles
FOR EASY RIDING

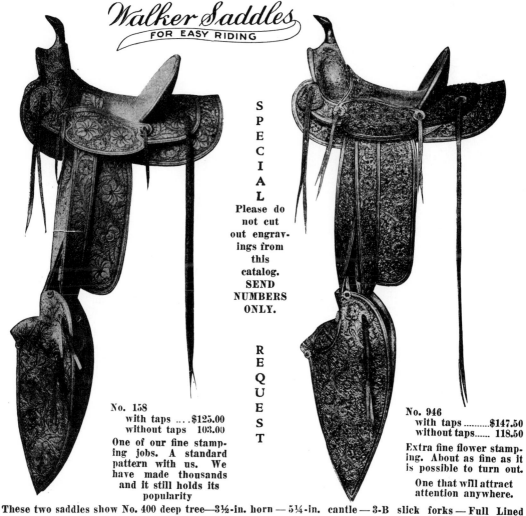

**S
P
E
C
I
A
L**

Please do
not cut
out engrav-
ings from
this
catalog.
SEND
NUMBERS
ONLY.

**R
E
Q
U
E
S
T**

No. 158
with taps $125.00
without taps   103.00
One of our fine stamp-
ing jobs. A standard
pattern with us. We
have made thousands
and it still holds its
popularity

No. 946
with taps $147.50
without taps...... 118.50
Extra fine flower stamp-
ing. About as fine as it
is possible to turn out.
One that will attract
attention anywhere.

These two saddles show No. 400 deep tree—3½-in. horn — 5¼-in. cantle — 3-B slick forks — Full Lined
We will be glad to build them on any tree you may prefer—no extra charge except that of $1.00 per inch
for swell forks over 12 inches.

For many years we have specialized on fine flower stamping, upon which our saddles stand in a
class by themselves. The art of flower stamping was brought to California at the time of Mexican
occupation and was here developed and perfected. Since that time California saddles have become
renowned for their superiority of their flower work which still holds good and this wonderful art
finds its highest expression in this fine work we show here.

WE MAKE A SPECIALTY OF FINE SILVER MOUNTED SADDLES AND BRIDLES

"Walker" since 1870

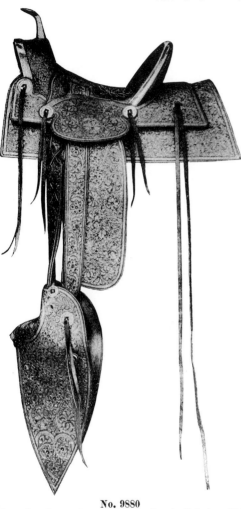

No. 9880

Extra fine flower stamped, full lined and stitched, quilted seat. With heavy sterling silver fork and cantle rims and conchos, silvered horn, with conchos on tapaderos.

A—As pictured above $241.00
B—As above, but less taps........................... 199.00
C—Stamped as above, with 24-inch tap-
    aderos, but no silver, and leather-
    covered horn 162.00
D—As above, without taps........................... 132.00

No. 360

No. 400 extra deep tree, 3½ inch horn, 5½ cantle 3-B fork, with fine quilted inlaid seat.

	With 26 in. taps	No. taps
No. 360—Extra fine Flower border stamp, as cut....	$123.00	$102.00
360-F—Full flower stamp....	129.00	106.50
360-C—Checker or basket stamp	104.00	88.00
360-B—Border stamp	101.00	85.50
360-P—Plain leather	99.00	84.50

Without quilted seat deduct $3.50

Walker Saddles
SINCE 1870

No. 159 Rose Stamp $110.00

12½ L. L. swell, 5¼ cantle, 3¼ horn

No. 160-A Silver conchas and liberty silver
 stirrups $132.00
No. 160-B No silver; iron-bound stirrups.... 117.00

TREE AND SADDLE BUILT TO YOUR ORDER, JUST AS YOU WANT IT, TO THE SMALLEST DETAIL

These fine rose stamp saddles are just about the handsomest saddles that are put up anywhere. They are built for the man who takes a pride in his outfit, and wants something better than the average.

   *   *   *   *

You know, the saddlery field has its "Lincolns" as well as its "Lizzies," each serving its purpose; but who rides in a "Lizzie" when he can afford a "Lincoln"?

   *   *   *   *

We have exceptional facilities for building fine sterling silver mounted saddles, bridles, martingales, etc., of which we have turned out a large number. If interested in something this type we will be glad to give you all the information at our command.

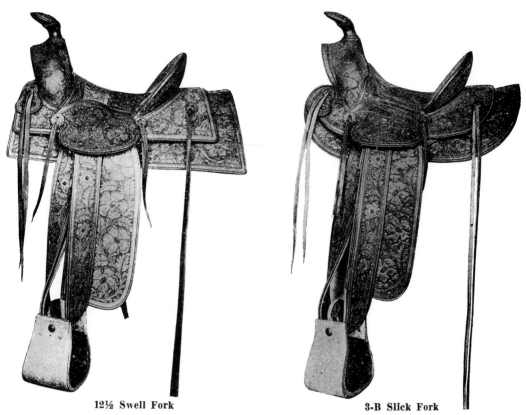

12½ Swell Fork   3-B Slick Fork

Famous Walkeroper Hand-Made Trees

3 inch Horn   3½ inch Head   4½ inch Cantles

TWO OF THE MOST ATTRACTIVE SADDLES WE MAKE

Extra-Fine Wild Rose Hand Stamping

No. 152 As shown, all lined $108.50	No. 154 As shown, all lined $102.50
152-C Check or basket, unlined............ 85.00	154-C Check or basket, unlined............ 80.00
152-B Border stamp, unlined................. 83.00	154-B Border, unlined.......................... 78.50
152-P Plain leather, unlined................... 81.00	154-P Plain leather, unlined 77.00

Above prices include stirrups up to 4 inches wide; 4½ and 5 inch stirrups 50c extra; 5½ inch stirrups $1.00 extra. Any of our saddles fitted with brass-bound, hand-made stirrups $1.00 extra; or bound with heavy liberty silver $2.00 extra; silver concha bolts in stirrups extra, $4.00 per pair.

TREES CHANGED TO SUIT YOU

(Do not cut out the engravings—send number only)

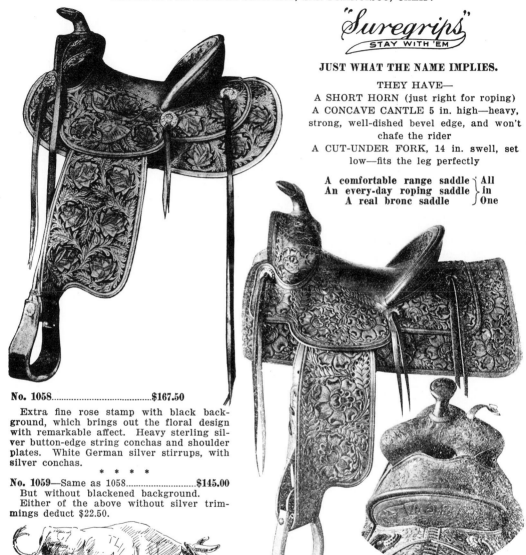

"Suregrips"
STAY WITH 'EM

JUST WHAT THE NAME IMPLIES.

THEY HAVE—
A SHORT HORN (just right for roping)
A CONCAVE CANTLE 5 in. high—heavy, strong, well-dished bevel edge, and won't chafe the rider
A CUT-UNDER FORK, 14 in. swell, set low—fits the leg perfectly

A comfortable range saddle } All
An every-day roping saddle } in
A real bronc saddle } One

No. 1058................................**$167.50**
Extra fine rose stamp with black background, which brings out the floral design with remarkable affect. Heavy sterling silver button-edge string conchas and shoulder plates. White German silver stirrups, with silver conchas.

* * * *

No. 1059—Same as 1058............**$145.00**
But without blackened background.
Either of the above without silver trimmings deduct $22.50.

No. 1051 Sure Grip	**$106.50**
1051-C Check and basket stamp	**91.00**
1051-B Border stamp	**89.50**
1051-Plain leather	**87.50**

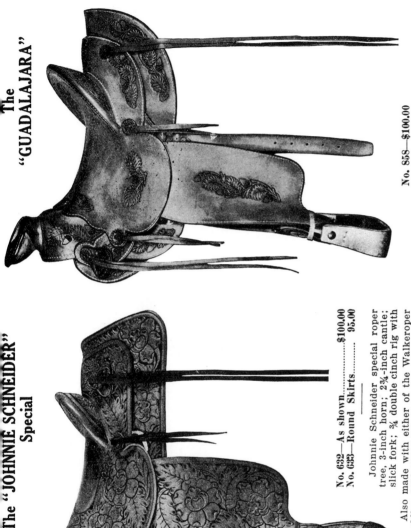

The "GUADALAJARA"

No. 858—$100.00

Cut shows 3-B Slim Fork. Made also with 12½ Walker Roper Fork, 4½-inch horn, 3½-inch cantle. Made any size desired. Showing the popular ¾ all-leather rig with flank cinch. FOR HOLDING A ROPE IT CAN'T BE BEAT!

The fork and horn are adapted from some Mexican saddles we imported from Guadalajara a few years ago, one of which we have kept in stock as a sample since that time. From time to time we have been called upon to make Americanized trees embodying these features which have proven very practical and useful when built into Walker Saddles, one of which we show here. Of course, this tree will be put in any of our saddles if desired. Extra charge $3.00.

The "JOHNNIE SCHNEIDER" Special

No. 632—As shown..........$100.00
No. 633—Round Skirts.......... 95.00

Johnnie Schneider special roper tree, 3-inch horn; 2¾-inch cantle; slick fork; ¾ double cinch rig with small flank rings. Also made with either of the Walkeroper forks shown in saddles 1072-1074-1076, if preferred.

This Tree and Saddle Designed and Made by us for JOHNNIE SCHNEIDER

The Champion Cowboy, winner of the highest honors in the Rodeos of the Rodeo Association of America, 1931; also scored almost 1000 points more than the winner of 1932.

He says: "This little saddle is what I've been wanting all my life. There are no changes that could be made to better it for roping, dogging and everyday use. It is light, strong, and rides a horse perfectly, and is the best roping saddle built. I ride it continuously and find it difficult to describe how much I like it, and every one else that rides it likes it as well as I do."

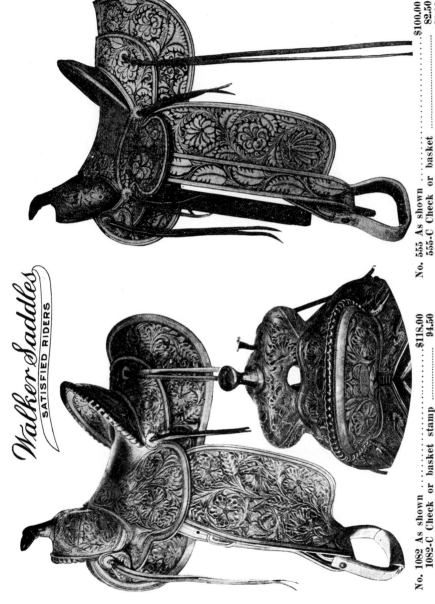

Walker Saddles — SATISFIED RIDERS

No. 555 As shown $100.00
555-C Check or basket 82.50
555-P Plain leather 80.00

Showing our No. 200 tree, 3 inch sloping horn, 5 inch cantle, 13 L. L. swell fork, centre fire, ¾ or Spanish rig with our new pattern flat bronze rings. One of our old veterans, tried and found not wanting.

Hundreds are in use all over this country, and the demand still keeps up for this most popular rig.

"YOU CAN'T KEEP A GOOD SADDLE DOWN!"

No. 1082 As shown $118.00
1082-C Check or basket stamp 94.50
1082-P Plain leather 92.00

Our famous "Salinas Tree," 15 inch swell, 3 inch horn, 5 inch cantle; rope bindings, extra dish. One of our strikingly handsome, new patterns—something out of the ordinary, and one of the prettiest saddles you have ever seen, and the most comfortable you ever sat in. As easy on your horse as it is on you. Its quality as good as its looks; a beautiful piece of flower work.
Without rope bindings, deduct....................$6.00

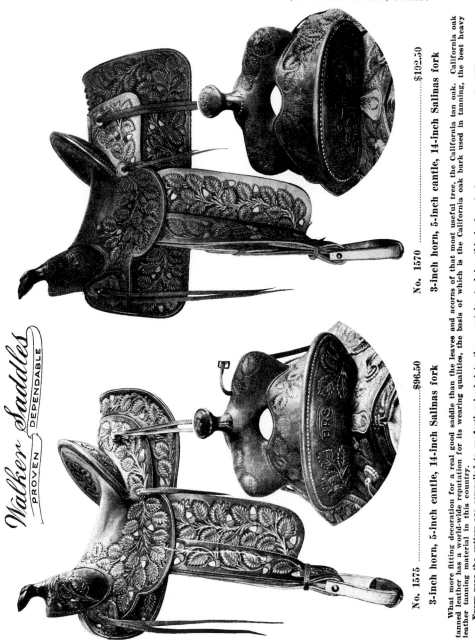

No. 1570 .... $102.50

3-inch horn, 5-inch cantle, 14-inch Salinas fork

What more fitting decoration for a real good saddle than the leaves and acorns of that most useful tree, the California tan oak. California oak tanned leather has a world-wide reputation for its wearing qualities, the basis of which is the California oak bark used in tanning, the best heavy leather tanning material in this country.

Every year the cutters are compelled to go further back into the mountains to bring this bark out—in many cases on pack saddles—greatly increasing the cost of production. For this reason some tanners use other barks and extracts to lessen the cost. But not so with our tanners. For 75 years they have used this California oak, and still do so regardless of its cost, and for nearly 60 years we have been using this leather. This largely accounts for the splendid reputation the Walker Saddles have for long service.

No. 1575 .... $96.50

3-inch horn, 5-inch cantle, 14-inch Salinas fork

Walker Saddles
PROVEN DEPENDABLE

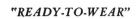

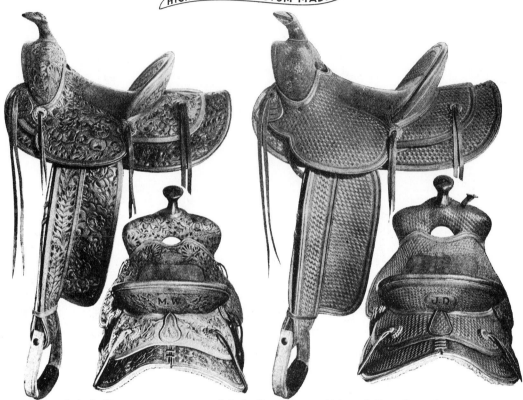

3 inch Horns   5 inch Cantles   14 inch Salinas Swell Forks

No. 932 Neat flower stamp..............................$94.00
Shown with the with the "straight around, no twist stirrup leathers, the most comfortable and durable style made. You'll like 'em!

No. 936 Full basket stamp................................$83.50
936-F Full flower stamp............................ 96.50
936-P Plain leather 80.50

These are carried in stock in the styles and dimensions shown on these two pages, and the trees run 14, 14½, and 15 inches in length. Other sizes made to order at short notice. They are rigged center-fire and three-quarter with flat bronze no-rust rings, or center-fire, five-eighths or three quarters rig with our flat plate, all leather rigging, $3.50 extra. They have your initials on back cantle, and any style cinch or stirrup, and can be shipped on five days' notice. *Be sure to give the length of tree and your height and weight.*

This will enable a man who has had his saddle wrecked, or has a chance to dispose of an unsatisfactory saddle to replace it immediately with the best in the land. For quick action use the Air Mail or Special Delivery letter, or fifty word night telegram. *We will take care of it in good shape!*

Walker Saddles
QUALITY FIRST—PRICE NEXT

"READY TO WEAR"
SOME NEW ARRIVALS IN THE WALKER LINE

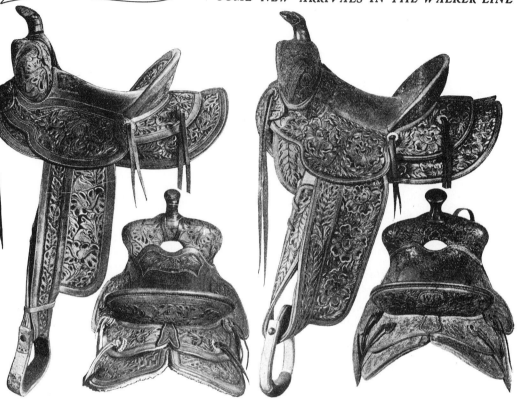

3 in. horn, 5 inch cantle, 14 inch Salinas fork

No. 940—A BEAUTY $95.50
Centre-fire, bronze ring rigging   (Changed to suit you)

No. 943—FULL FLOWER $100.00
Three-quarter, all-leather rigging

As to quality—there is no question—our best materials and efforts go into these saddles

Not "ready-made" in the usual sense of the term, which implies a factory-made, piece-work job. Saddles of this type being made to sell at a price and the quality pared down to meet that price. "READY TO WEAR" means strictly high-grade saddles, built of our very best material, by our best saddlers with all the pains-taking care and under the strictest personal supervision, that have made the reputation of our saddles what it is. For many years, it has been our practice to build our saddles on the custom plan, but having had so very many urgent calls for saddles for quick shipment we are now taking care of this demand with our READY TO WEAR line, carried in stock in 14, 14½, and 15 inch trees.

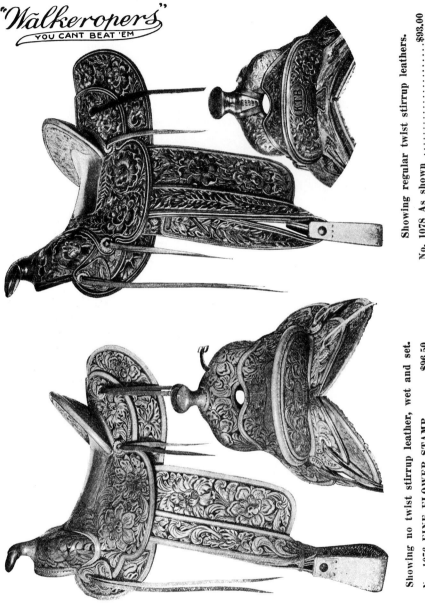

"Walkeropers"
YOU CANT BEAT 'EM

Showing no twist stirrup leather, wet and set.

No. 1076 FINE FLOWER STAMP $96.50
1076-C Check or basket stamp 81.00
1076-B Border Stamp 80.00
1076-P Plain leather 78.50

Showing regular twist stirrup leathers.

No. 1078 As shown $93.00
1078-C Check or basket stamp 79.50
1078-B Border Stamp 78.50
1078-P Plain leather 77.00

Built on our Walkeroper tree No. 1—3 inch horn—3½ inch head—4 inch cantle—12½ inch swell fork—with good spread, setting down snug on the withers, giving it a firm hold on the back and yet so constructed that it will not hurt the withers—the common failing of roping trees. To be had in 14, 14½ and in 15 inch trees. Other sizes and any combination of these horns, forks or cantles that you may desire. Built

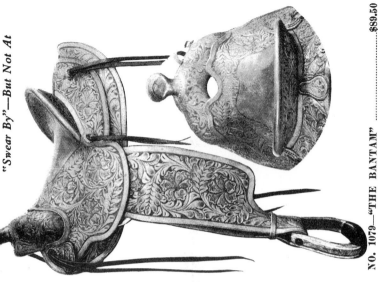

"WALKER'S"—The Saddle You
"Swear By"—But Not At

Walker Saddles
SATISFACTION

NO. 1079—"THE BANTAM" $59.50
(Only 30 pounds)
A tough little fighter and a Samson in strength
A handy "one-hand" saddle

Our best hand-made Walker tree, 3-inch horn, 12½-inch fork, and 3-inch cantle. Made 3½ or 4-inch cantle if you wish. Cinch riggings, latigoes, cinch regular weight, the balance of the stock selected from our No. 1 light-weight California oak tan hand stuffed leather, the best in the world, and a nice job of flower stamping to finish it off.

No. 1079-c—Checker or Basket Stamp........**$80.00**
No. 1079-p—Plain Leather........**$77.00**

No. 1580—Oak leaves and acorns........**$86.50**

Walkeroper tree, 3-inch horn, 4-inch cantle, 3-B fork. A saddle of highest grade of materials and corresponding workmanship, with simple but tasty decorations—for the man who does not care for a lot of expensive stamping but wants the best of everything else.

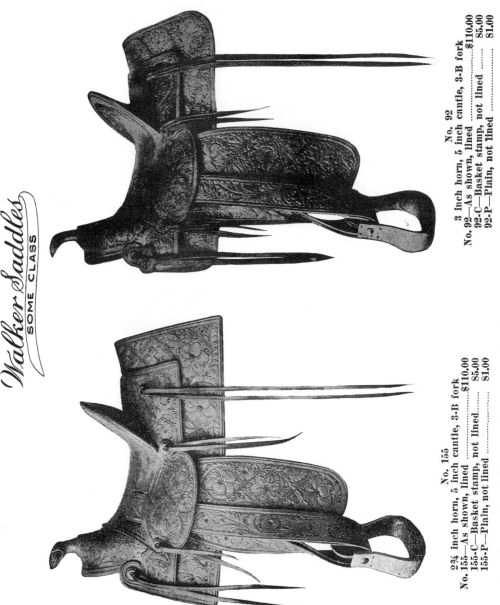

Walker Saddles
SOME CLASS

No. 92

3 inch horn, 5 inch cantle, 3-B fork
No. 92.—As shown, lined $110.00
92-C.—Basket stamp, not lined 85.00
92-P.—Plain, not lined 81.00

No. 155

2¾ inch horn, 5 inch cantle, 3-B fork
No. 155.—As shown, lined $110.00
155-C.—Basket stamp, not lined 85.00
155-P.—Plain, not lined 81.00

Two of our finer-grade saddles. Examine the stamping closely—it will bear inspection. We often hear it said, "You can always tell a Walker flower stamp saddle by its stamping—it's different." Quality materials and workmanship, of course.

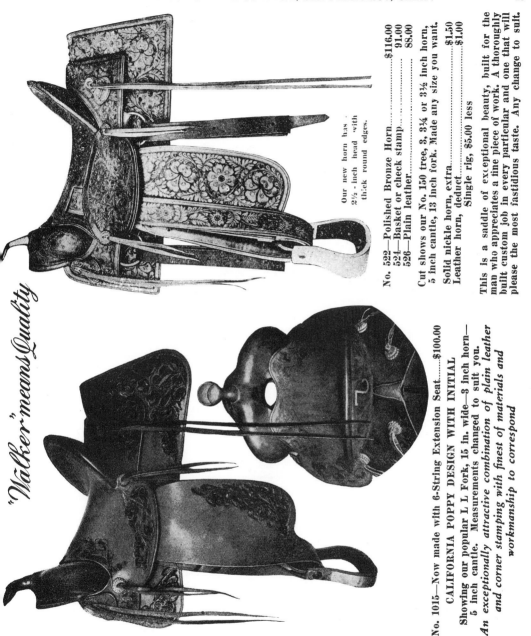

"Walker" means Quality

Our new horn has 2½-inch head with thick round edges.

No. 522—Polished Bronze Horn..................$116.00
524—Basket or check stamp.................. 91.00
526—Plain leather.................. 88.00

Cut shows our No. 150 tree, 3, 3¼ or 3½ inch horn, 5 inch cantle, 13 inch fork. Made any size you want.

Solid nickle horn, extra..................$1.50
Leather horn, deduct..................$1.00
Single rig, $5.00 less

This is a saddle of exceptional beauty, built for the man who appreciates a fine piece of work. A thoroughly built custom job in every particular and one that will please the most fastidious taste. Any change to suit.

No. 1015—Now made with 6-String Extension Seat......$100.00

CALIFORNIA POPPY DESIGN WITH INITIAL

Showing our popular L L Fork, 15 in. wide—3 inch horn—5 inch cantle. Measurements changed to suit you.

An exceptionally attractive combination of plain leather and corner stamping with finest of materials and workmanship to correspond

Walker Saddles
GOOD CLEAR THROUGH

TWO POPULAR STYLES IN THE ROUND CORNER SQUARE

This one a popular priced rig.   This one especially handsome with flower stamp
stirrup leathers.

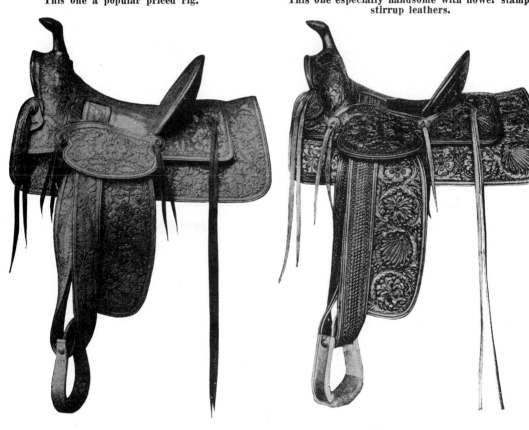

No. 43
3 inch horn, 5 inch cantle, 3-B fork
No. 43—As shown $98.50
    43-C—Check or basket 85.00
    43-B—Border stamp 83.00
    43-P—Plain leather 81.00

No. 192
3 inch horn, 5 inch cantle, 12 inch LL fork
No. 192—As shown $100.0
    192-X—With flower stamp stirrup
        leathers 106.0
    192-C—Check or basket..................... 85.0
    192-B—Border stamp 83.0
    192-P—Plain leather 81.0

Walker Saddles
NO SORE BACKS

No. 688	No. 725
A low priced, full stamped saddle, with highest grade materials and workmanship.	A very pleasing combination of plain leather and scroll work—more expense in materials than adornment.

No. 688
3 inch horn, 5 inch cantle, 12½ inch LL fork

No. 688—Price as shown $90.00
   688-C—Checker or basket stamp 80.50
   688-B—Border stamp 79.00
   688-P—Plain leather 77.50

No. 725
3 inch horn, 4½ cantle, 3-B fork

No. 725—Price as shown $84.00
   725-C—Checker or basket stamp 80.00
   725-B—Border stamp 78.50
   725-P—Plain leather 77.00

Don't overlook our offer to make any changes in trees or leathers you may desire.

PLEASE DON'T CUT OUT THE ENGRAVINGS—Send the numbers only of the articles wanted.

Walker Saddles
'NOUGH SAID

No. 958—Fine flower stamp......................$100.00
    958-C—Checker or basket................. 86.50
    859-B—Border stamp.......................... 85.50
    958-P—Plain leather 84.00

Another of our handsome new designs built on our
No. 100 tree, with 15-inch LL swell Fork, 3-inch
horn, 5-inch cantle, and fitted with our all-leather
flat plate rigging which eliminates ring sores.
Ring rigging $3.50 less if preferred.

NOTE!

*Our All-leather flat plate rigging as shown
on saddle No. 958 applied to any of our
saddles at an extra cost of $3.50.
Can be had in either the center-fire five-
eighths or three-quarters rig.*

No. 93—Full Flower stamp.........................$92.50
    93-C—Check or basket stamp............. 80.00
    93-B—Border stamp............................... 78.50
    93-P—Plain leather 77.00

Built on our No. 100 trees, 3-inch horn, 5-in
cantle, 3-B slick fork. This is one of our old-tir
favorites which still holds its own with any of the

NOTE!

*Our improved flat "Norust" bronze rigging
rings are so constructed that they lay flat in
the riggings. No hump in the center or wea
on the edges of leather. They also lay fla
on the skirts and if you have ring trouble
we recommend these.*

It may be that none of the trees we show exactly suit you—in this case, just select the horn out of o
tree, the fork of another, and the cantle of another, and make any change in the leathers and stampir
that you may prefer, and we will make your rig just that way—and **THERE IS NO EXTRA CHARG**
FOR IT. Sixty-four years of experience are at your service.

Walker Saddles
NOT HOW CHEAP-BUT HOW GOOD

No. 390

A handsome design, combination of plain leather and fine flower work, 3¼ inch horn, 5 inch cantle, 13 inch LL fork, six-string extension seat.

No. 390—Flower border stamp, as cut....$96.00
    390-F—Full flower stamp 100.00
    390-C—Checker or basket stamp........ 82.50
    390-B—Border stamp 81.00
    390-P—Plain leather 79.50

No. 157

**EXTRA SMALL LEATHERS, ALL LINED
AND STITCHED**

Flower stamp as shown....................$99.50   **$119.00**
Basket stamp, not lined...................... 79.50   **94.00**
Border stamp, not lined...................... 78.50   **92.50**
Plain leather, not lined...................... 77.00   **90.50**

If you don't just fancy the trees shown in these or any of our saddles, we will be glad to make any change you wish.

"Walkeropers"
SURE HOLD 'EM

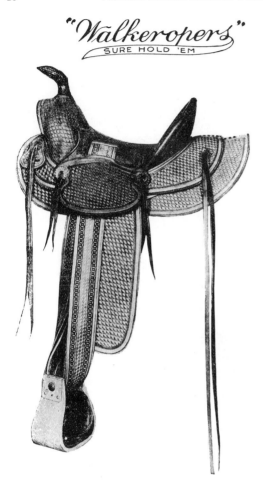

No. 203

2¾ inch horn, 4 inch cantle, 3-B fork
Stirrups up to 4 inches wide

No. 203—As shown	$80.00
203-F—Full flower	92.50
203-P—Plain leather	77.00

"Walkeropers" have made a name for themselves, second to none. You don't take any chances when you buy one of these rigs.

No. 119

2¾ inch horn, full slope 3½ in. cantle, full slope

3-B fork

	With 26 in. taps	No taps
No. 119—As shown	$ 96.00	$80.00
119-F—Flower stamp	115.00	92.50
119-B—Border stamp	92.50	78.50
119-P—Plain leather	91.50	77.00

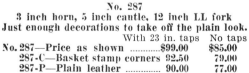

No. 287		No. 137	
3 inch horn, 5 inch cantle, 12 inch LL fork		3 inch horn, 4½ cantle, 3-B fork	
Just enough decorations to take off the plain look.		A novel effect in a flower panel border.	

	With 23 in. taps	No taps
No. 287—Price as shown $99.00	$85.00
287-C—Basket stamp corners 92.50	79.00
287-P—Plain leather 90.00	77.00

	With 26 in. taps	No taps
No. 137—Price as shown $110.00	$91.00
137-C—Basket stamp panels 100.00	82.00
137-P—Plain leather 92.00	77.00

THESE TWO ATTRACTIVE SADDLES HAVE MORE MONEY PUT IN THE INSIDE THAN THE OUTSIDE.

"*Walkeropers*"
YOU CAN'T BEAT 'EM

"READY TO WEAR"

Carried in Stock for quick shipment in 11½ and 15 in. length

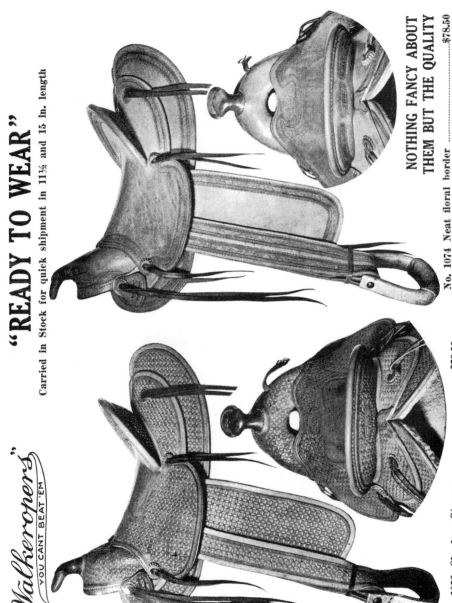

NOTHING FANCY ABOUT THEM BUT THE QUALITY

No. 1074 Neat floral border $78.50
1074-F Full flowered stamp 92.50
1074-C Check or basket stamp 79.50
1074-P Plain leather 77.00

Walkeroper Tree, extra low 3½ in. horn, 3½ in. head, 3 in. cantle, 10 in. swell fork; 2½ in. cantle if desired.

No. 1072 Checker Stamp $79.50
1072-F Flower Stamp 92.50
1072-B Border Stamp 78.50
1072-P Plain leather 77.00

Walkeroper Tree, low type, 2¾ inch horn, 3½ inch head, 3½ cantle, 11 inch swell fork.

SHOWING STRAIGHT AROUND, NO TWIST STIRRUP LEATHERS—THEY'RE ALL TO THE GOOD

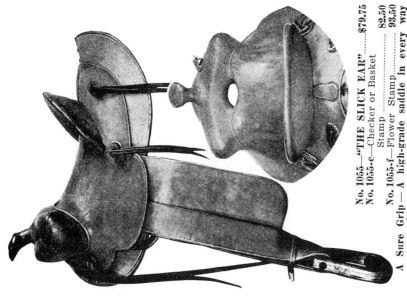

No. 1055—"THE SLICK EAR"......$79.75
No. 1055-c—Checker or Basket
           Stamp 82.50
   No. 1055-f—Flower Stamp 93.50

A Sure Grip — A high-grade saddle in every way with no money spent in adornment

Our famous low sure-grip tree, 2½-inch horn, 14-inch fork, 3¾-inch cantle. Any changes you desire made. Made to fill the demand for an all-round work saddle. Low roping horn, fork and cantle, with enough undercut to afford a sure seat when you need to ride a rough customer.

We make 'em fancier but no better.—The most useful saddle on your ranch.

This is where the WALKER CUSTOM SERVICE comes in. We own and operate our own custom saddle and tree shop, all under one roof, and our complete equipment enables us to offer you a service that you cannot get anywhere else. Will you take advantage of it? IT DOESN'T COST ANY EXTRA.

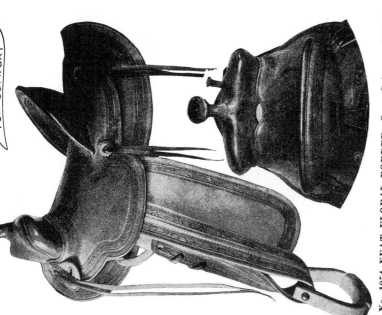

"Suregrips"
FOR COMFORT

No. 1054 NEAT FLORAL BORDER—Sure Grip $82.50
1054-P PLAIN LEATHER—Sure Grip 81.50

To the man who wants quality and durability in preference to decoration this rig appeals.

Just take note of the saddles and trees with which you are familiar. How many of them suit you exactly? Probably not one. If there is one thing that the experienced cowman is cranky about, it is his tree—which must not only fit him, but his horse as well. It is not always an easy matter to get just the right thing out of ready-made trees and saddles. Right here is where

Eight "Walker Association" saddles made for two big California Rodeos: Salinas and Livermore.

These two rodeos are run by experienced cattlemen, who know a good saddle when they see it. With their knowledge of the reputation of the Walker saddle, for long and hard service, it is very natural that they should select the best there is for their rodeos, and the old-established and time-tested Walker was their choice. Read what they say about them.

Visalia Stock Saddle Company,
2117 Market Street,
San Francisco, California.

Gentlemen:

It is with great pleasure that we express to you our appreciation of the manner in which your firm has filled the order for the eight contest saddles for our show.

These saddles conform in every particular to the rules as laid down by the Rodeo Association of America and are entirely satisfactory to the contestants. We wish to compliment you on their construction and material, and we want to particularly recommend the flank cinches, for they are especially good from the humane stand point and for bucking-horse contest, and far superior to the ordinary flank rig.

Trusting we have the pleasure of seeing you at our next show, with best wishes, we remain.

LIVERMORE STOCKMEN'S RODEO.
Your very truly,
By Hugh S. Walker,
Arena Director.

HSW/P

THE BEST IN THE WEST SINCE 1870

No. 912—Association saddle, with buck strap as shown **$75.00**

Wool-covered, elastic flank cinch $2.50 extra

Made on our best grade, hand-made tree, 14 inch swell fork, 5 inch cantle, with stirrup leathers, riggings, latigoes and cinch, first-class; balance of stock regular Association weight about 32 pounds. This type of saddle is used by practically all the Rodeos out West.

Visalia Stock Saddle Company,
2117 Market Street,
San Francisco, California.
Gentlemen:
The eight Bronc Riding Contest saddles you made for us have been subjected to very severe tests and are highly satisfactory, both to us and to the riders. We can fully recommend your saddles to anyone.
With best wishes,
Yours very truly,
CALIFORNIA RODEO.
AH:VL   By Arthur Hebbron, President.

Walker Saddles
"HEAP GOOD"

TRICK SADDLE

The tree is specially made in our own shops, rawhide covered, every detail worked out to give the utmost aid, comfort and service to the rider. Low cantle with heavy roll, full quilted seat, built just right for this work. A fine job of flower stamping with the highest grade of materials and workmanship to correspond.

Just about one of the most handsome saddles you ever saw for trick work, built to the order of a well-known trick rider, May Greer, who pronounces it perfect for her work.

Read her letter and see what she says about it.

Furnished with a heavy round leather sling on off side for trick work.

No. 1200—As shown $125.00
1200-C—Checker or basket stamp 110.00
1200-B—Neat border stamp 107.50

VISALIA STOCK SADDLE CO.
Gentlemen:

My Visalia trick saddle is a dandy. It has a good high horn, the right height cantle, good heavy rigging and everything is put together right. If anyone is figuring on buying a new trick riding saddle, I would certainly suggest they buy a Visalia. It can't be beaten for the money or for twice the price. If I ever need another one I will get it from Visalia.

Yours truly,

MAY GREER.

DUDE RANCH SADDLES

To provide for a growing demand created by a rapidly increasing form of pleasure and recreation, we have developed these three styles of saddles for the use of Riding Clubs and Dude Ranches and for both men and women riders.

They are built on rawhide-covered trees, out of our California oak-tan leather, are light, strong, easy riding and comfortable, and priced right.

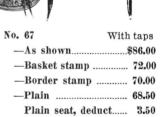

No. 71—   With taps
—As shown $79.00
—Basket stamp...... 66.50
—Border stamp...... 64.75
—Plain 63.00
Quilted seat, extra   3.50

No. 67   With taps
—As shown.....................$86.00
—Basket stamp 72.00
—Border stamp 70.00
—Plain 68.50
  Plain seat, deduct...... 3.50

No. 787—27 lbs...............$47.50

NOTE—Although the cuts are small, these saddles are full adult size in all their measurements, the trees being 14 in., 14½ in., and 15 in. long.

THESE SADDLES

are well constructed with well-shaped, comfortable seats; skirts lined with bark tan woolskin; iron bound oak stirrups, good, strong latigoes and strings. They are well built and will stand long and continued service.

Short tapaderas extra $4.00.

DUDE RANCH SADDLES

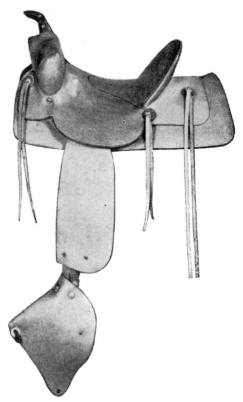

No. 783—25 Pounds

Plain leathers, slim fork tree, center fire, good strong riggings and latigoes, hair cinch, 1½-inch half-double stirrup leathers to buckle. $38.50

Swell fork tree $1.50 extra

No. 795—29 Pounds

Rawhide covered tree; 12-inch swell fork, as shown...$47.50

Less tapaderos, with iron-bound stirrups 44.00

THESE SADDLES ARE EQUIPPED WITH OUR QUICK-CHANGE BUCKLE STIRRUP LEATHERS, HAIR CINCH AND LATIGOES.

Made of our best leather. Light weight and easy riding. Trees and leather are full adult size.

NOTE: We carry a complete line of English and polo saddlery. Write for catalog.

"Walker" since 1870

BOYS' SUREGRIP SADDLE

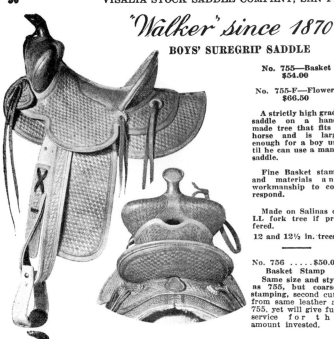

No. 755—Basket
$54.00

No. 755-F—Flower
$66.50

A strictly high grade saddle on a hand-made tree that fits a horse and is large enough for a boy until he can use a man's saddle.

Fine Basket stamp and materials and workmanship to correspond.

Made on Salinas or LL fork tree if prefered.

12 and 12½ in. trees

No. 756 . . . . . $50.00
Basket Stamp
Same size and style as 755, but coarser stamping, second cuts from same leather as 755, yet will give full service for the amount invested.

No. 1080 . . . . . $47.50

With swell fork
$50.00

Without taps—$3.00 less

A strongly built saddle on a hand-made, rawhide covered tree; quilted seat, wonderfully easy riding for men or women.

Plain seat $3.00 less

The average boy is full of life and "pep" and what better outlet for his surplus energy than a good saddle and outfit, one that he can call his own. Its use will take up his spare time and give him a training along the lines of what will probably be his life work, and make him useful and proficient in the work of the ranch.

3-B Fork
2 inch Horn
3½ inch Cantle
Price $45.00

No. 161—Boys' Saddle
Good rawhide covered Tree

Finest grade of tan saddle leather on a rawhide covered tree, all bronze trimmings. A fine little saddle for hunting and fishing trips and for resorts. Easy to pack around.

No. 1100

Army saddle; brand new Genuine U. S.

$12.50

PACK OUTFITS   KYAX

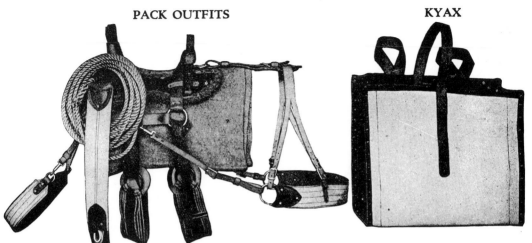

Showing No. 20 Outfit.
Blankets not included.
No. 10 Outfit.
Very best grade throughout, extra heavy saddle leather straps, all hand copper-riveted and heavy wax thread sewed. Used by professional packers, miners, prospectors and sheep men all over the West. They wear for years.

    Single Rig............$25.00   Double Rig.........$28.00
This rig has forked breastplate running to cinch.

No. 20 Outfit.
One grade lighter than No. 10 rig and a great favorite with many packers. Same grade material as No. 10, and will give you good service.

    Single Rig............$21.00   Double Rig.........$24.00
No. 30 Outfit.
Our light rig, made of the best materials, but lighter than No. 20, extensively used by hunters and campers, and others doing light packing.

    Single Rig............$16.50   Double Rig.........$19.50

Showing No. 10, made of the very heaviest canvas the mills produce. Extra heavy leather ends, ears and straps. Substantially put together by hand; copper rivets. Will last a life time.
Per pair......................................$22.00

No. 20.—Heavy weight canvas with extra heavy bottoms, leather lined, sewed with heavy linen thread and copper riveted. A good durable article. Per pair........$14.50

No. 30.—Medium weight canvas well sewed and copper riveted. Solid leather ears and straps. Will give good service. Per pair
-- $9.50

Any special or particular style built to order.

Visalia Tree

Everything Hand Copper Riveted
NO IRON MACHINE RIVETS in
any of our Outfits.
They rust and rot the leather and canvas.

No alum leather used—
Oak Tanned leather only.
Same as used in our Stock Saddles

Humboldt Tree

OF COURSE—We know that you can buy, and also we can make, cheaper outfits than these. But do they pay? Alum or cheap harness leather, iron machine rivets, etc., cannot make a durable piece of work. A man up in the high mountains or out in the desert, miles from nowhere, with a broken-down pack rig, is just plum out of luck. **OUR RIGS WILL GET YOU THERE AND BRING YOU BACK, AND WILL DO THIS YEAR AFTER YEAR. IT PAYS TO USE GOOD STUFF! WE MAKE IT!**

"Walkeropers"
SURE HOLD 'EM

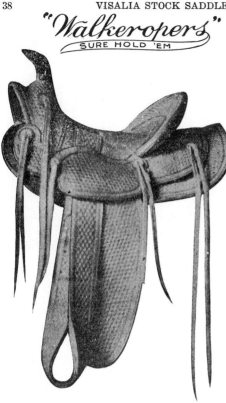

THE IDEAL ROPING SADDLE
No. 214, with stirrups any style
Shown with regular twist stirrup leathers

Our old-timer, since 1894—Just as
popular as ever!

2¾ horn — 3 inch head — 4 inch cantle
3 B slick fork

No. 214—Basket Stamp	$80.00
214-F—Flower Stamp	93.00
214-B—Border Stamp	78.50
214-P—Plain Leather	77.00

"WALKEROPERS"

These saddles, designed primarily for heavy roping, are the result of many years' experience in building this type of trees and saddles. For all these years we have enjoyed the benefits of having our own tree shop, where we could carry on experiments, aided by suggestions from practical, experienced cowmen, who know the requirements for a real cowman's saddle. Thus we have been able to bring our trees and saddles up to the high standard they have attain.

The horns are just the right height and pitch for roping, with large heads, rawhide bound to withstand the hard usage they receive in this work.

The cantles are low, of various heights to suit every taste, and bindings are buck sewed by hand, greatly outwearing the thread sewed cantles.

The forks are of various widths and shapes, but all set low, fitting snugly down into the withers, where the tree gets its hold on the horse's back, yet so constructed that they clear the top of the withers, being free from the common failing of that type of tree, many of which will hurt a high-withered horse at that point.

Every point in these trees and saddles has been carefully worked out, with the result that for practical usefulness and service and maximum wearing qualities the "WALKEROPER" line stands preeminent.

Most of this line are shown with the "HALF DOUBLE NO TWIST" stirrup leathers which we highly recommend for comfort and long service.

When moulded as shown, there is no hump at the ankle to cause discomfort, no twist or friction to wear out the stirrup leathers—they lay smooth to the leg and are the slickest thing out in the way of stirrup leathers.

Just say in your order—"Half double, no twist", and we will do the rest. Contrary to the prevailing custom *we make no extra charge for double leathers if you want them.* Fitted with centerfire, or three-quarter ring rigging. All leather flat plate center-fire, five-eighths or three-quarter rig, $3.50 extra. Initials or brand on back cantle no extra charge.

There's a vast difference between factory-made and custom-made work. Factory-made goods are turned out almost entirely by piece work, rushed through to "make time," the sole object seemingly to be to see how cheaply they can be produced. Custom work is generally made by day work, and no incentive exists to crowd the work through at a speed which is detrimental to the quality of the goods, and the natural result is a more substantial and thoroughly made article than is usually produced by the piece-work method.

Our goods are all HAND CUSTOM MADE by day work, the idea being "not how cheap, but how good." This, and the use of the finest and most expensive materials, accounts for the extreme durability for which they are noted.

Every week, we repair Walker Saddles from 10 to 25 years old and still doing good service

CINCHES USED ON OUR SADDLES

MANE HAIR CINCHAS

Selected stock; well sewed leathers. The best cinches put on any saddle. Our own make.

DOUBLE RIG—IN PAIRS

No. 20 $6.50 Cotton and Leather.

No. 19 $5.50 Hair and Web

Any combination of hair, mohair, fishcord, web or leather you may desire.

LEATHER FLANK

ARIZONA STYLE

No. 27 .. $2.50

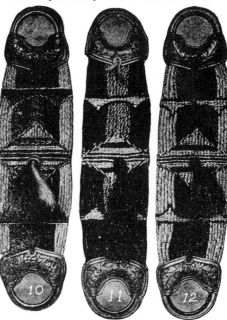

OUR CINCHES

are all hand made from good, clean, long stock, well spun and twisted, with tassels. The mohair cinches are very popular, being soft yet strong and durable.

Our bronze rings, being rust proofed, add greatly to the life and safety of the cinch.

Our well - known oak-oil latigoes are worthy running mates to these fine cinches

Tackaberry Buckle— 35c. Phosphor bronze —$1. Our own make, extra heavy bronze for heavy wide rings —$1.50.

SINGLE RIG

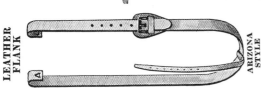

No. 13 $4.50 No. 16 $4.00 No. 18 $4.00 No. 15 $4.50
Hair—Fine Hair or Mohair Cotton 4 to 7 inch
Any width, 4 to 7 inch—Bronze rings, 50c extra.

EXTRA FINE
Bronze Rings

FINE
Steel Rings

MEDIUM
Steel Rings

NEW BRONZE RINGS

Size	No. 10	No. 11	No. 12
4 in.	$6.50	$5.00	$4.50
5 in.	7.00	5.25	4.75
6 in.	7.50	5.75	5.00
7 in.	8.00	6.25	5.25

Round
in any cinch $1.00 ea.

Flat

If you want one of these finer cinchas on your saddle, deduct $4.00 from these prices and add the difference to price of saddle.

Unless otherwise ordered we send all single rig saddles with 6-inch, No. 16 Cincha; ¾ rigs with 5-inch, No. 16 Cincha; Spanish rigs with 4-inch, No. 16. State your preference, if any.

Cut showing styles of cinch leathers. Sent full leathered if not specified.

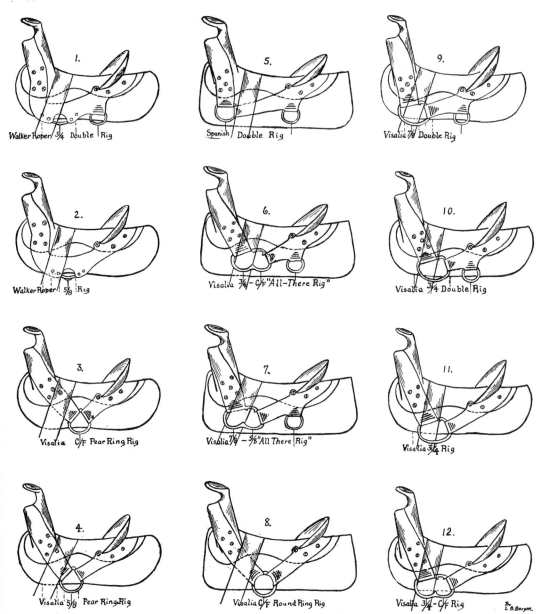

1. Walker Roper 3/4 Double Rig

5. Spanish Double Rig

9. Visalia 7/8 Double Rig

2. Walker Roper 5/8 Rig

6. Visalia 3/4 - C/F "All-There Rig"

10. Visalia 3/4 Double Rig

3. Visalia C/F Pear Ring Rig

7. Visalia 7/8 - 5/8 "All There Rig"

11. Visalia 3/4 Rig

4. Visalia 5/8 Pear Ring Rig

8. Visalia C/F Round Ring Rig

12. Visalia 3/4 - C/F Rig

L. B. Bergen.

CINCH RIGGING PRICES

Rigging rings as shown in cuts Nos. 3, 4, 8 and 11 are regular types of rings which we ordinarily use in our saddles, so kindly state which you prefer.

If other combinations are wanted, add prices quoted below to the prices in the catalog.

Walkeroper ¾ double as in cut No. 1........$6.00
Walkeroper ⅝, as in cut No. 2............... 3.50
Double rigs as in cuts Nos. 5, 9 and 10........ 2.50
Visalia All There Rig, as in cuts No. 6 and 7... 4.00
Visalia ¾-centerfire, as in cut No. 12.......... 1.50

These prices are for saddle with single cinch and two latigoes. If saddle is wanted with front cinch and extra back cinch, two latigoes and two single billets, add $3.00

If wanted with Arizona flank cinch and one single billet, add $2.50

Unless otherwise instructed, when saddle is ordered with double rig as in No. 5, 9 or 10, we will send the saddle with front cinch, Arizona flank cinch, two latigoes and one single billet.

THREE-QUARTER RIG   (See Cut No. 11)
Our Improved Flat Rigging Rings

Notice how far forward the stirrup leathers swing, to the full extent of the groove in the tree, and owing to the extra length of the ring, there is also plenty of backward swing, without binding the stirrup leathers.

Flank rings $2.50 per pair extra, put in.

Most riders know that a heavy piece of leather fitted into a round ring will, when the strain is put on it, adjust itself to the curve of the ring. This throws nearly all of the strain on the edges of the leather, causing it to wear through in time, particularly if the ring is of the thin, flat type. This also causes the leather to hump up in the center, making a lump there that many times makes a ring sore, and also is uncomfortable for the rider.

You will readily see that the parts of these improved rings where the leather lays are straight, not curved, so that the strain is put evenly the whole width of the strap. This eliminates the wear and strain on the edges of the straps, adding to the life of the riggings, and also cutting out the lump, as these rings make the least bulk of any rings in the market. They are made of the toughest and strongest no rust metal known, and are the ideal rings for your saddle.

CINCH RIGGINGS

About the most prolific source of trouble from a saddle is ring sores, and about the most difficult to combat, for a rig that works well on some horses, may not work on others.

TRY THIS FOR RING TROUBLES

Flank Rings on this rig $2.50 extra

OUR IMPROVED ALL LEATHER FLAT PLATE CINCH RIGGING

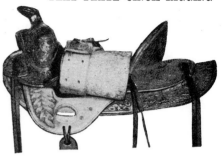

This is the rigging you need for your saddle and you cannot realize the pleasure and comfort derived from riding in a saddle with the stirrup leathers swinging free, without interference from the cinch rigging or rings, until you try one. It relieves your horse from the discomfort of working under a rig that annoys or hurts him, and both horse and rider will do their work with less fatigue than with any other rigging.

Cut from the heaviest prime leather, well stretched and fitted, reinforced by our improved thin, flat, non-corrosive plates, which leaves the rigging flexible so that it will adjust itself to the shape of the horse.

The openings for the latigoes are strengthened by an extra clip covering the edge of the leather and plate, affording a smooth running edge for the latigo slightly curved just enough to allow for the adjustment of the saddle on the horse so the latigoes will pull true. This opening is below the edge of the skirts, so that the latigoes lay off the skirt on the blanket, taking the pressure off the skirts.

Another valuable feature is that the lower stirrup leathers come out from under the tree, and pass OVER the cinch rigging, instead of under it as with the ring rigging, so there is no pressure whatever on them from the rigging, and leaving them free to swing the whole length of the space between the tree and the rigging, as the cut shows. Made center fire, ⅝ or ¾ rig, $3.50 extra.

OUR NEW "WALKEROPER" RIGGING

Here is a cinch rig that works on them all—the last word in cinch riggings.

This new device consists of a rustless steel plate securely attached to the leather cinch rigging. It is so constructed that the wraps of the latigoes lay in a recess or groove on the under side, flush with the metal with no lump to cause the trouble sometimes made by the ordinary rigging rings.

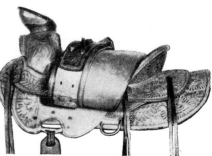

THE POPULAR ¾ DOUBLE RIG

All the metal is Rustless Steel. This rigging, as shown, with cinch and two latigoes, costs $6.00 more than the regular ring riggings. (See Cut No. 1, page 40.)

Leather flank cinch complete—$2.50 extra.

Also made in ⅝ and ¾, without flank rings. $3.50 extra on any ring-rigged saddle.

TAPADERAS

We are the original inventors of the "Visalia" one piece "Tap," the best and most durable **Tap** in the market. No stitching to rip. Made of heavy prime leather and with plenty of foot room. We will furnish any of the styles shown on our saddles at the prices quoted on this page.

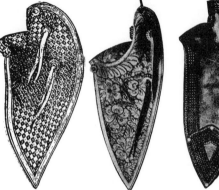
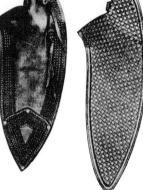

Regular length 23 inch.

Flower stamped, as shown, 18 in.	$17.00
Flower stamped, as shown, 21 in.	18.50
Flower stamped, as shown, 23 in.	19.50
Flower stamped, as shown, 24 in.	20.50
Flower stamped, as shown, 26 in.	22.50
Basket or check stamp, 18 in...	13.00
Basket or check stamp, 21 in...	14.00
Basket or check stamp, 23 in...	14.50
Basket or check stamp, 24 in...	15.00
Basket or check stamp, 26 in...	16.00
Basket border stamp, 18 in.....	12.75
Basket border stamp, 21 in.....	13.50
Basket border stamp, 23 in.....	14.00
Basket border stamp, 24 in.....	14.50
Basket border stamp, 26 in.....	15.50
Plain, 18 in.................	12.50
Plain, 21 in.................	13.00
Plain, 23 in.................	13.50
Plain, 24 in.................	14.00
Plain, 26 in.................	15.00

REGULAR PATTERN   **LAKEVIEW PATTERN**
Long Taps for Show.
Short Taps for Protection.

DOUBLE POINT
Flower Stamp..$3.00
Basket Stamp.. 2.75
Plain 2.50
Add to list prices.

ROUND POINT PATTERN

OUR EXCELSIOR TAPS.   **LACED TAPS.**

Shallow.   Medium.   Medium   Deep.

Any of these Taps made shallow, medium or deep, as preferred.

EXCELSIOR TAPS
Made of one solid piece of stock, with an extra heavy toe piece running over the nose, clear under to the heel, buck sewed on, two seams. This stiffens and strengthens them. Practically indestructible.

THE TAP FOR HARD SERVICE.

Flower stamp	$19.00
Basket or check stamp	14.00
Border or plain	13.50

LACED TAPS.
All our short Taps are made of heavy prime stock, cut in one piece, and fit the stirrup at the heel, leaving no room for mud and slush to drive in. Being lined with wool sheepskin, they keep the feet dry and warm—the real purpose of a Tapadero.

Flower stamp	$16.50
Basket and check stamp	12.00
Border and plain	11.50

When ordering Taps of any kind separate, always give the width bottom stirrup they are intended for.

PROTECTION FROM WET AND COLD IN WINTER, AND FROM BRUSH ALL THE YEAR ROUND
See parcels post chart on back page for postage rates

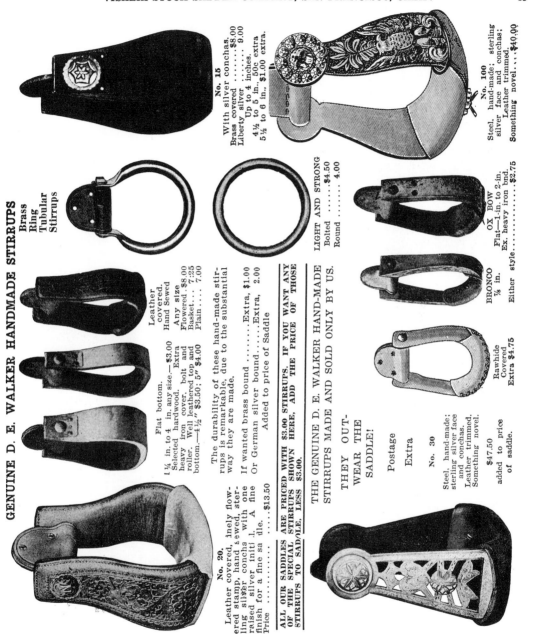

GENUINE D. E. WALKER HANDMADE STIRRUPS

Brass Ring Tubular Stirrups

No. 15

With silver conchas.
Brass covered $8.00
Liberty silver 9.00
Up to 4 inches.
4½ to 5 in. 50c extra
5½ to 6 in. $1.00 extra.

No. 100

Steel, hand-made; sterling silver face and conchas; Leather trimmed. Something novel...$40.00

Leather covered. Hand Sewed

Flat bottom.

1¼ in. to 4 in. any size.—$3.00 Selected hardwood. Extra heavy iron cover, bolt and roller. Well leathered top and bottom.—4½" $3.50; 5" $4.00

Any size
Flowered $8.00
Basket... 7.25
Plain.... 7.00

The durability of these hand-made stirrups is remarkable, due to the substantial way they are made.

If wanted brass bound ....Extra, $1.00
Or German silver bound....Extra, 2.00
Added to price of Saddle

No. 20.

Leather covered, inely flowered stamp, hand sewed, sterling silver concha with one raised silver initi l. A fine finish for a fine sa dle. $13.50

ALL OUR SADDLES ARE PRICED WITH $3.00 STIRRUPS. IF YOU WANT ANY OF THE SPECIAL STIRRUPS SHOWN HERE, ADD THE PRICE OF THOSE STIRRUPS TO SADDLE, LESS $3.00.

THE GENUINE D. E. WALKER HAND-MADE STIRRUPS MADE AND SOLD ONLY BY US.

THEY OUTWEAR THE SADDLE!

Postage Extra

No. 30

Steel, hand-made; sterling silver face and conchas. Leather trimmed. Something novel.

$47.50 added to price of saddle.

LIGHT AND STRONG

Bolted $4.50
Round 4.00

OX BOW

Flat—1-in. to 2-in.
Ex. heavy iron bnd.
Either style............$2.75

BRONCO

⅞ in.

Rawhide Covered Extra $4.75

GENUINE "WALKER" HAND-MADE TREES

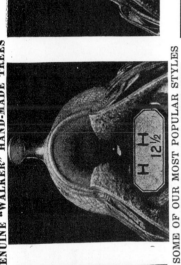
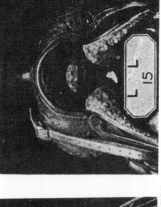
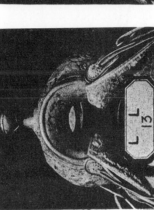

F F 11

H H 12½

3 B

L L 15

L L 13

K K 12½

SOME OF OUR MOST POPULAR STYLES

"WALKER" TREES STAND THE TEST

Double Rawhide Covered Trees $5.50 Extra

RICK'S BUCK HORN TREE 15" SWELL

Our Popular Salinas Rodeo Swell Fork

Showing 15 in. swell. Made 12 to 16 in. swell.

Special Notice

Unless specified in the order, we use the regular 3-B fork in all our saddles not shown with swell fork.

No extra charge for swell forks up to 12 inches. Over 12 inches, charge extra as follows: $1.00 per inch for flower stamped; 75c per inch for all others.

Back bulge, 50c extra on all trees.

Be sure to describe fully the tree you want in your saddle. This is important, and lack of this information will cause delay in getting your order out.

We are the only saddlers in the United States making all our own saddles, trees, and stirrups.

We make a specialty of building new trees to replace broken or defective trees in old saddles. If the leathers are in good condition, they are worth a new tree. WE CAN DUPLICATE ANY TREE MADE IN THE UNITED STATES.

GENUINE WALKER TREES—HAND-MADE

**3 inch straight horn
5 inch cantle**

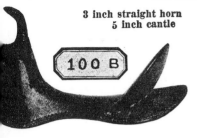

100 B

**3 inch half sloped horn,
5 inch cantle**

150 B

**3 inch full sloped horn,
5 inch cantle**

200 B

Our old standbys for many years the most popular styles we made, and they still retain their hold on our trade. With our fully equipped tree shop, we are ready to build your tree to your order just as you want it in every particular.

No. 1
12 ½ in.
Swell fork
4 in. cantle

No. 2
10 ½ in
fork
3 ½ in.
cantle

No. 3
9 in. 3-B
fork
3 in. cantle.
Heads from
3 to 4 ½
inches.

Short
Horn,
3 inches
with
Head Up

3B Fork
4½-inch
Cantle

Medium
Slope

Round
thick
edges,
solid
bronze
$2.00
extra;
solid
nickel,
$2.50
extra.

Double
rawhide
over the
fork for
extra
strength.

**Walkeropers"
Nos. 1, 2 and 3**

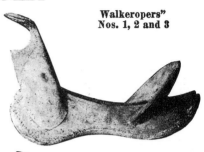

WEATHERLEY TREE

650 B

**POLISHED
METAL HORN**

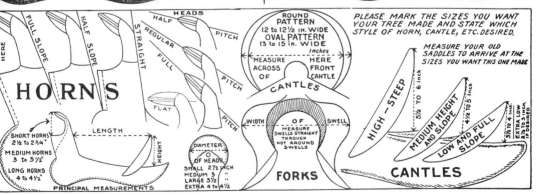

DIRECTIONS FOR ORDERING SADDLES. (SEND FOR ORDER BLANKS.)

PLEASE DO NOT CUT THIS CATALOG—SEND THE NUMBERS ONLY OF THE ARTICLES.

As all these details are important, to enable us to understand your order as you intend it, and to build the work to conform to your ideas, we ask you to read these pages carefully. For rush orders, use the 50 word night telegram.

We ship saddles and heavy packages by express or parcel post, as desired, and we can now send shipments up to $200.00 value and 70 pounds weight to any post office. The rates are about equal on long hauls, but in favor of the parcel post for short distances and on small packages. We use the lower rates in all cases. Goods sent C. O. D. to money order offices only —to other post offices the value of goods and postage must accompany order.

WE REQUIRE A DEPOSIT OF 25 PER CENT ON ALL ORDERS. Use U. S. or express money orders payable to Visalia Stock Saddle Co., San Francisco (not Visalia). Personal checks accepted for collection.

1—NUMBER OF SADDLE. Write plainly, so there will be no mistake.

2—TREE. Be SURE to state length, also state style wanted. If not specified, we send style shown in cut of saddle. If you prefer something different, do not fail to state so.　　　　**See page 45 for Tree Measurements**

3—RIDER. Give your height and weight, and size shoe worn. This enables us to get the stirrup leathers and rosaderos the right length, and send the right size stirrup.

IF SADDLE IS WANTED DIFFERENT FROM CUT, see items following. When describing parts of a saddle or tree, do not say, "small or large," as that is too indefinite, but specify "long or short," "narrow or wide," "high or low." This refers particularly to horns, cantles, bastos, rosaderos, etc., and if measurement in inches can be sent, or a paper pattern, so much the better.

BASTOS OR SKIRTS If saddles shown with round skirts are wanted with square skirts, add $4.00 for plain skirts, $5.00 for basket or checker stamp, and $6.00 for regular grade of flower stamp, as in saddle No. 93.

5—CANTLE—Most of our saddles are shown with the "bound" cantle, with a heavy leather or rawhide binding. We also make the FULL ROLL cantle, with 1½-inch projection, and the HALF ROLL, made the same as the full roll, but only ¾-inch projection; $1.00 extra charge for either.

6—HORN. We usually send our saddles out with the COVERED horn, but if preferred, we send them HALF COVERED, or with both neck and head BARE, in which cases we double rawhide the unleathered parts, giving double the wear in roping.

RIGGING AND CINCHES. We make three styles of SINGLE RIGS. (See pages 40 and 41).

The regular CENTER FIRE, as most of the saddles are shown, with 6-inch, No. 16 cinch.

The ¾ RIG, as on saddle 151, with 5-inch No. 16 cinch.

The SPANISH RIG, as on saddle 555, with 4-inch No. 16 cinch.

Prices all the same. Should you prefer other cinches, see page 41, and state which you prefer.

DOUBLE RIG, as shown as No. 522, sent out with No. 19 cincha, unless otherwise ordered; $5.00 extra added to price of any single rig SADDLE. In addition to the above we make the various combination rigs shown on page 40. On all our flower stamp saddles, you may have your choice of the very best forged steel rings, leather covered, or our special non-corrosive metal rings, the toughest metal of its class yet discovered. All of the other saddles are fitted with the steel rings, but if the non-corrosive rings are wanted, add 75 cents per saddle.

All our cinch riggings are extra wide, from extra heavy cuts of the very best prime stock in the hide, well stretched, all hand-laced into the rings and will wear for years. All single rig saddles are sent out with latigoes on each side. If desired with double billet on off side, with buckle tongue in cinch, state so in order. No extra charge.

All double rig saddles sent out with latigoes on near side and double billets on off side, with buckle tongues on both ends of cinchas. If desired different state so in order.

We also furnish the Arizona style flank cinch—a 1½, 1¾ or 2-in. strap laced into the flank ring on offside, with a buckle on other end, and a short billet in flank ring on near side.

8—TAPS. Saddles will be sent as shown, unless otherwise ordered. If you desire a different pattern or length tap, describe what is wanted, and we will furnish any other style you may prefer. (See page 42.)

9—STIRRUP LEATHERS. Made in three styles, price the same.

WYOMING HALF DOUBLE—single over tree, double through stirrup, with lacing showing front. (See saddle No. 958.) Most of our saddles are shown with the regular twist in the stirrup leather, but on some styles we show and we strongly recommend the "straight around, no twist," wet and moulded to make the stirrup set right. Just say 'no twist, wet and set." No hump to chafe the ankle, no friction between the leathers, securing longer service and more real comfort than any other style. (See saddles No. 940 and 1076.)

CAL. HALF DOUBLE—Same as above, but with concealed lacing at top of rosadero. This is adapted only to solid seat saddles. Outward appearance same as the 3-4 double leathers.

3-4 DOUBLE—Twice around tree and stirrup, sewed and riveted to bottom of rosadero, and concealed lacing at top of rosadero. See saddle No. 158—called "full double" by some riders.

Standard width of stirrup leathers FULL 3 inch, not scant, as is often the case. If desired wider, add 50 cents per ¼-inch over 3 inches. Our stirrup leathers and cinch riggings cut from No. 1 prime stock.

10—STIRRUPS. The saddles are shown with various sizes and styles of stirrups, and it will be important to specify what you want. See page 43.

11—ROSADEROS or FENDERS. You may have some particular pattern that you like which we will make if preferred to that shown; otherwise will send as cut shows. One piece rosadero and stirrup leathers like No. 1050, extra $3.50

12—WEIGHT. Time was that a saddle was not considered amounting to much unless it weighed round fifty pounds—an erroneous idea, that has been proven as such by actual experience. The most progressive riders are no longer willing to burden their animals with these clumsy and cumbersome rigs, but are demanding lighter weight saddles, thirty-five pounds and under. Our rigs will average about as follows:

Regular weight, round cut single rig...33 to 35 lbs.   Light weight, round cut..............30 to 33 lbs.
Regular weight, square cut, single rig...35 to 37 lbs.   Light weight, square cut..............32 to 34 lbs.
according to size of tree and leathers.

Double rig adds about 2 pounds, heavy swell forks and double rawhide from 1 to 3 pounds, short taps 4 pounds, long taps 5 to 6 pounds, according to length. We find that the hides from smaller and finer bred animals produce leather of the finest grain, the toughest fiber, and make the most durable stock, far superior in wearing qualities to the stock made from the heavy, coarse grained, rough hides. The effects of the elements, the successive wetting and drying, and the action of wind and sun and alkali, are far more destructive to leather than the actual wear, which the finer grade stock is more able to withstand. Our long experience and close observation of the old saddles that come to us from time to time for repairs has proved to us conclusively that the medium weight saddles, when cut from prime stock, as ours are, will actually outwear those made from the heavy "bull hide" stock. For this reason, we recommend the medium weight saddles, BUT, if you prefer a heavy saddle we are here to make it, and will furnish just what your order calls for.

13.—THE SEAT. A most important item to consider, for an easy seat is a source of great comfort to a rider, and upon it depends his ability to perform his work with the least amount of fatigue, while a hard riding saddle is a perpetual source of discomfort and bad language.

The ordinary ready-made saddle has a seat built like the rest of the rig, in the most economical way, the foundation being a metal plate with insufficient leather above it to properly shape the seat, saving both time and leather, the result being the misshapen and uncomfortable seats for which this class of saddles is notorious.

The ease and comfort of the Walker saddle seat is proverbial, the result of the solid and painstaking way in which they are built, neither time nor leather (both expensive) being spared in that part of the work. This gives us a seat that is properly shaped, comfortable and positively will not sink, and which cannot be obtained by the "economical" method mentioned.

If you wish the metal plate or strainer, we will put it in, if so ordered, in addition to our regular seat, without extra charge.

STYLES OF SEATS.

¾ SEAT. Extending just beyond stirrup leathers, leaving a hand hold between front edge of seat, and bottom of fork.

FULL SEAT, extending beyond the stirrups leathers up onto the fork, covering opening below fork (made both plain and quilted.) Made either solid or looped, as ordered.

LOOP SEAT. Cut for stirrup leathers to loop through after passing under seat jockeys.

Most of our saddles are shown with the ¾ loop seat, cut for stirrup leathers to loop through after passing under seat jockeys. But as most riders prefer the solid seat, we are making them that way unless ordered as shown in cut.

SOLID SEAT, not cut for stirrup leathers, which do not show after passing under the side jockeys. Preferred by many as tending to keep water, dust, etc., out of the blankets.

QUILTED SEATS. Ours are padded soft, made of the very finest, heavy colored pigskin scroll stitched with heavy silk, and inlaid, buck sewed at point of wear, and are the most comfortable and durable quilted seats put in any saddles, and a decided addition to the appearance of the rig. Either ¾ or "full quilted" seat, $3.50 extra, on saddles shown with plain seats.

¾ Solid quilted seat shown in saddle 360.   ¾ loop seat shown in saddles 159-160
Full solid seat shown in saddle 154.   ¾ solid seat shown in saddle 555.

EXTENSION SEAT. See saddle No. 390. Allows full forward swing to stirrup leathers. No strings or buttons at base of fork to interfere with the knees. $2.00 extra on any saddle. Not adapted to slick fork saddles.

STATE YOUR PREFERENCE. BUT IN FUTURE IF ORDER DOES NOT SPECIFY WE WILL MAKE ALL SEATS ¾ SOLID AS IN SADDLE 555.

14—INITIALS OR BRAND. When so ordered, we stamp either of these in the leather and if you send the impression of your iron, we will reproduce it exactly. WRITE INITIALS PLAINLY, and state whether to go on back or front of cantle or other location. No charge.

15—OILING. If so ordered, we oil saddle with absolutely pure neatsfoot oil, not doped with fish oil or other cheap substitutes. No charge.

BLACKING. When saddles are ordered in black leather, we accomplish this by a method that leaves the leather soft and pliable like harness leather, a black that won't wear red in a short time. The usual shop method of treating the leather with strong chemicals to make the blacking "take" burns and ruins the stock, which accounts for the prejudice against black saddles. Extra charge $2.50. With taps $3.00.

16—ROPE STRAP. We furnish all saddles with buckle rope strap on off side of fork, or with split for horn, if preferred. If a second strap or string is desired on the opposite side of the fork, add 75 cents. Quirt snaps put on the left rear seat strings, if ordered. No charge. Latigo holders go with all saddles.

SPECIAL NOTICE

WE OWN AND OPERATE ON OUR PREMISES THE ONLY SADDLE TREE FACTORY IN THE STATE OF CALIFORNIA. WE HAVE THE DISTINCTION OF BEING THE ONLY SADDLE MAKERS IN THESE UNITED STATES WHO CAN MAKE YOUR SADDLE TO YOUR ORDER WITH A CUSTOM MADE TREE, MADE TO YOUR OWN IDEAS, AND WITH OUR OWN MAKE HAND-MADE STIRRUPS AND CINCHAS.

EVERY EXPERIENCED RIDER HAS HIS OWN VIEWS REGARDING HIS TREE AND THE KNOWING ONES ARE NO LONGER SATISFIED TO TAKE THE READY-MADE TREES USED IN OTHER SADDLERY SHOPS IN THE WEST, BUT WANTS HIS TREE MADE HIS OWN WAY, TO SUIT HIM AND NOT SOME ONE ELSE, AND WE ARE EQUIPPED TO MAKE IT FOR HIM.

SO, MR. PARTICULAR RIDER, SEND IN YOUR ORDER AND LET US SHOW YOU WHAT WE CAN DO. SEND IN YOUR SKETCHES AND MEASUREMENTS, AND WE WILL GIVE YOU JUST WHAT YOU WANT. DON'T OVERLOOK THE IMPORTANCE OF THIS FEATURE OF OUR SERVICE.

SEND FOR ORDER BLANKS

VISALIA STOCK SADDLE COMPANY

In these days of quick changes in the cost of materials, and in view of the absolute uncertainty of what may transpire in the future, we are unable to tell just how long the prices quoted in this catalog will hold good. For that reason, THESE PRICES ARE SUBJECT TO CHANGE WITHOUT NOTICE, and if it is possible to lower our prices we will be only too glad to give you the benefit of whatever saving may be possible, and if manufacturing costs increase, we shall have to advance our prices accordingly. At all times we shall keep the prices as low as we can and still keep up our high standard of materials and workmanship.

If at any time you are in doubt as to the current prices of our goods, please write and state what you are in need of, and we will be glad to quote you the present prices on goods shown in catalog No. 31.

We call especial attention to the beautiful and artistic designs of flower stamping in Saddles, not equalled by any other line in the United States.

Saddle Fittings

	Price	Insured Post. Extra
The famous Visalia Latigoes, best oak oil-tan:		
1½ inch, $1.50; 1¾ inch, $1.75; 2 inch, $2.00; 2¼ inch ____ $ 2.25		20c
Double billets or tugs, heavy Saddle Leather:		
1¾ inch, $1.25; 2 inch, $1.40; 2¼ inch ____	1.55	15c
Saddle Strings, our best oak oil-tan, per set ____	1.85	15c
Buttons, per set ____	.15	07c
Stirrup Leathers, with strings, 3 inch, half double, with points, plain, per pair $7.50; with points, basket stamped, per pair, $8.00; with points, flower stamped, as in No. 93 ____	11.50	35c
Double Stirrup Leathers, extra ____	1.00	
Finer grades of flower stamping, as in No. 160, extra per pair ____	1.50	
Finer grades of flower stamping, as in No. 946, extra per pair ____	2.50	
Rope Strap, with buckle ____	.40	
Leather Horn Wraps ____	.50	
Rosaderos, or fenders, 7¾x18 inches, plain $4.00; basket or checker stamp, ____	5.00	
Flower stamp, like No. 93 ____	7.50	
New skirts, lined with best grade of wool skins, approximately 14x28 inches		
Square, plain leather, $16.50; basket or checker stamp ____	18.25	
Flower stamp, as in No. 93 saddle ____	24.75	
Round, plain leather, $12.50; basket or checker stamp ____	14.00	
Flower stamp, as in No. 93 saddle ____	18.00	
New wool skins installed in round skirts ____	6.50	
New wool skins installed in square skirts ____	7.00	
New Visalia tree fitted in old leathers ____ $25.00 to 30.00		
New centerfire ring installed in your saddle ____	7.50	
New all-leather flat plate rigging installed ____	11.00	
New Walkeroper rigging with flank dees, installed ____	14.50	
Saddle restrung throughout ____	3.50	

NOTE: *We prepay the postage on hats, boots, bits and spurs when full amount of the purchase price accompanies the order. For postage on other goods, consult the parcel post chart on back page of catalog*

CALIFORNIANS: Do not overlook the California State tax of 3% when sending in your remittance.

CORONAS   **SADDLE BLANKETS**

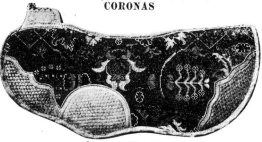

Coronas No. 10

Brussels carpet with woolskin lining, leather safes and binding, made to fit saddle or the pattern you send.

Round...............$11.00   Square.............$11.50

No. 5

Heavy curled hair, soft and porous, leather safes, not bound.

Round................$5.00   Square................$5.50

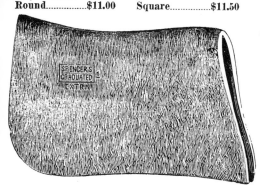

Graduated Felt Blankets

No. 75—Gray, round...$3.50
78—Gray, Square 4.00

Extra heavy wool washables, fit our saddles and will not wrinkle.

No. 200—Brown, extra fine wool (Three Fold....$4.75
225—Brown, heavy (Single) 1.75
230—Brown, heavy (Two Fold)...................... 3.25
250—Blue, extra heavy (Three Fold)............ 3.75
275—Blue (Two Fold) 2.75

GENUINE NAVAJO INDIAN BLANKETS

No. 1—Best quality, per pound..........................$2.15
2—Fine quality, per pound............................ 1.90
3—Good quality, per pound.......................... 1.65
Weights from 3½ to 7 lbs.—Double fold.

While the first cost on Navajo Blankets is greater, the longer service and greater satisfaction they render offset the cost. These blankets fit our saddles.

"Walker" means Quality

THE CALIFORNIA PANTS

No. 100-S

Shirt.............$6.50

Same color to
match No. 100
pants, but reg-
ular shirt
weight

BE SURE TO
SEND SIZE

FINE FUR CALF VEST

No. 1—Flower Stamp....$22.00
No. 2—Basket Stamp.... 20.00
Plain leather binding on edge instead
of facing—**$15.00**

Since
1870

No. 914
Button front, notched collar. Belt
and top all of same material.

These coats are made of natural tan calf skin, which can be washed with pure Castile soap
and water. Length of coats is 30 inches.

No. 915
Zipper front, no buttons, and can be closed
to the neck. Belt of same material.
Price of No. 914, $12.00; No. 915, $12.50

No. 100—$13.50
(Delivered)

These pants are made
extra heavy, of pure wool,
so closely woven that it
is practically wind and
rain proof. A rider wear-
ing a pair of these pants
and a No. 100-S shirt and
jacket is equipped to defy
any weather he is liable
to meet this side of the
north pole.

The color is dark brown
plaid.

We also carry the same
style and color as No. 100
but of lighter weight.
Price **$7.00**

"THAT'S MY BRAND"

LEE

– 101 –

COWBOY OVERALLS

RULERS OF THE RANGE

The Overall with Snap and Kick
They Wear — They Fit

Made of Lee Denim — That Heavier,
Tougher Fabric

Copper Rivets in Front — Thread Rivets
on Hip Pockets — Assuring you that your
saddle will not be scratched or marred

Lot 101 —Cowboy Overall, 10-oz. Denim........................$1.75

Lot 101J—Cowboy Jacket, 10-oz. Denim........................$1.95

Lot 131 —Cowboy Overall, 8-oz. Denim........................$1.45

Here's a Jacket that'll bring joy to the heart of every cowboy
and cowman. Made of the same cloth used in the 101 overall.
Roomy and comfortable — yet snug and convenient. Pleated
Front — Breast Pocket — Rust Proof Buttons. Every Lee Garment Guaranteed — Your Money Back If Not Satisfied.

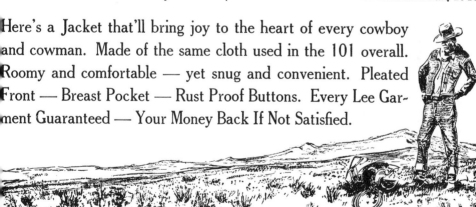

ANTI - FIRIN

THE MARVELOUS ABSORBENT

USED by some of the best-known Veterinary Surgeons, Horse and Cattle Breeders, Logging Contractors, Race Horse Owners and Polo Players, Riding Academies, Kennel Owners and Ranchers.

In Preference to Firing or Blistering

for the removal of all Bony or Fleshy Enlargements as Ringbones, Sidebones, Curbs, Bone and Blood Spavin, Splints, Big Knees, Shoe Balls, Inflammation of the Hoofs, Strained Tendons, Barbed Wire Cuts, Harness Sores, Wounds, Running Withers and Bow Tendons on horses.

Half Pints
35c

Pints
60c
each

WATERPROOF
PRESERVER
FOR
Boots and Shoes

The finest waterproofing we have yet found for boots, leather chaps and all kinds of leather work; also fine for ropes and riattas.

FOR THE DAIRY
Cake Bag
Lump Jaw
Sore Udders
and Teats
Wire Cuts
Rheumatism
and Lameness.

For Many Human Ailments
Running Sores
Sprains
Swellings
Rheumatism
Lameness
Ring Worm
Poison Oak

ANTI-FIRIN
REMOVES WITHOUT
FIRING — BLEMISH
OR PAIN

Large Cans, $2.50 postpaid, cash with order
Small Cans, $1.50 postpaid, cash with order

BICKMORE'S GALL CURE
This well-known article needs no recommendation from us. It does the work.
2-oz. can..................35c
6-oz. can..................75c
For saddle and collar galls it has no equal.

PROPERT'S SOAP
Used in all the stables where fine saddlery is kept. Nothing better made
Per can..................75c

A little time and labor in washing and oiling your riding equipment will pay big dividends in the greater comfort and longer service it will give you.

The action of sweat, alkali and the elements will in time affect the best of leather, and cause it to become dry, bony and brittle. Stirrup leathers and latigoes are the parts most affected, and many a man has had a bad spill from a neglected latigo breaking unexpectedly. This reminds us that the Walker oak-tanned latigoes outwear them all.

ABSOLUTELY
PURE
NEATSFOOT
OIL
NONE BETTER
WE USE IT ON OUR
SADDLES
PUT UP BY
VISALIA STOCK SADDLE Co.
SAN FRANCISCO

Pints
40c

Quarts
70c

We buy this direct from the manufacturer in quantities. We use it on our work and know it is good.

RAWHIDE REATA

We cannot always furnish the exact length ordered, so make your remittance to cover an extra foot or more and save possible delay thereby.

SPECIALLY PRICED—30c per foot
Light, Medium or Heavy
(If not specified we send medium)

These are all hand made of selected No. 1 stock, carefully prepared, skillfully braided, and no imperfect strands worked in. Thirty-four years' record backs them up. Will outwear a dozen grass ropes.

Made from the finest and longest fiber produced in the Philippines. Smooth and of great strength. The every day rope of the Western Cow Man.

THE FAMOUS PLYMOUTH ROPE

Without doubt the finest and strongest Manila rope made. Three strand, full sizes.

3-8-inch, light, per foot..............4½c
13-32-inch, medium, per foot..........5½c
7-16-inch, heavy, per foot 6½c
Without Hondas, cut any length you wish.

Brass Honda put in 75c
Rawhide Honda, put in 75c
Rope Honda, rawhide lined 50c

HONDAS

Rawhide 75c

Brass Oval ..25c

HONDAS

Put in Manila ropes.

Brass 75c
Rawhide . 75c
Knotted Honda Rawhide lined—
50c

HOGUE'S
Handy Honda
25c

SAMSON COTTON SPOT CORD, THE STANDARD ROPE FOR SPINNING.

No. 10—5-16-inch light spinning, per ft..........4c
No. 12—3-8-inch medium spinning 5c
No. 14—7-16-inch, heavy, roping 6c
Ropes Waterproofed 25c extra

HAIR ROPE

THESE PRICES FOR LIGHT AND MEDIUM SIZE ROPES.
HEAVY ROPES COST 10 PER CENT EXTRA

Made In Mixed Colors

WITH HEART—22 FT.

Mane		Tail	
No. 50	.........$6.00	No. 60	.........$4.50
No. 55	.... 7.00	No. 65	.... 5.00

WITHOUT HEART—22 FT.

Mane		Tail	
No. 70	.........$5.00	No. 80	.........$3.50
No. 75	.... 6.00	No. 85	.... 4.00

Tie ropes 12 ft. long 2-3 above prices.
Tie ropes 16 ft. long ¾ above prices.

MEXICAN IXTLE ROPES

A fine grade, remarkably strong and smooth. For trick and calf roping.

No. 1 Grade—$3.00

RATTLER ROPE

The strongest and smoothest rope made. Pure linen — Won't wear rough. 7-16 in diameter. 11c a foot for heavy work. 3-8 in. diameter 9c a foot for ordinary work.

SADDLE BAGS   **BRANDING IRONS**   **LEATHER POCKET**   **FENCE TOOL**

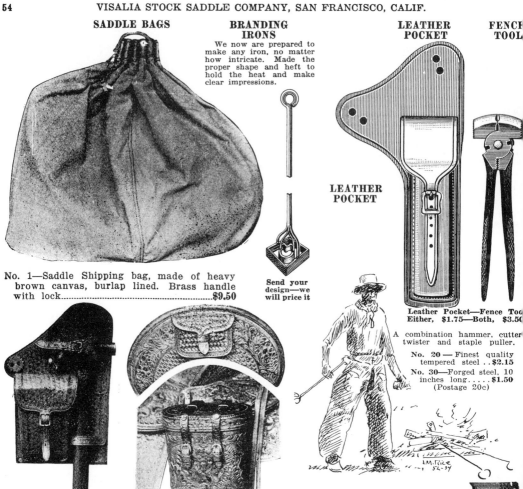

We now are prepared to make any iron, no matter how intricate. Made the proper shape and heft to hold the heat and make clear impressions.

No. 1—Saddle Shipping bag, made of heavy brown canvas, burlap lined. Brass handle with lock..**$9.50**

Send your design—we will price it

LEATHER POCKET

Leather Pocket—Fence Tool Either, $1.75—Both, $3.50

A combination hammer, cutter twister and staple puller.

No. 20 — Finest quality tempered steel ..**$2.15**
No. 30—Forged steel, 10 inches long.....**$1.50**
(Postage 20c)

HAMMER AND STAPLE CARRIER

To tie on saddle, back of cantle:
Basket stamp $3.00
Plain leather.......... 2.50
Flower stamp.......... 5.50
Made also to carry pliers in place of hammer. Same price.
NOTE: Tools not included in price.

CANTLE WALLET ON BACK OF CANTLE

Basket stamp.............................$2.25
Flower stamp............................. 3.00

FIELD GLASS CARRIER

Protect your glass and have it handy
Basket stamp.............................$8.00
Flower stamp............................. 9.50
Heavy saddle leather and handsewed. Made to go on any part of saddle or carry on shoulder

SADDLE POCKETS

Detachable as shown:
No. 35—Plain............$ 7.25
No. 35—Basket.......... 7.50
No. 60—Flower.......... 11.50

If made on the jockeys.
No. 35—Plain...............$5.25
No. 55—Basket............ 6.00
No. 60—Flower............ 8.75

THE CARE OF A HORSE

Due to our modern life, many people are not familiar with the care of animals. These suggestions are submitted in the hope that they may be found interesting, helpful, and stimulating to further study. A person not accustomed to the use of the horse may not recognize the symptoms of sickness until well advanced. An experienced caretaker observes his horses carefully and will detect the slightest lameness or abnormality at once.

FEEDING—The primary object of feeding is the preservation of health and the maintenance of condition in order that the individual may perform the work for which it is intended. Foods may be grouped as: Flesh-making; fat, heat, energy producing; bone-making; fibrous or bulky materials; and water. Naturally, some foods will serve more than one purpose, but some classification is desirable to better understand good feeding practice. In general, the chief flesh-making foods for horses are: Oats, corn, barley and alfalfa. Those that serve for bone-building are rich in mineral elements, especially calcium and phosphorous. These are particularly important for young growing animals. The bulky, fibrous foods have relatively less nutritional value but are necessary for the normal functions of the digestive tract of herbivorous animals. Water has little nutritive value but is necessary for body maintenance.

A good food must contain constituents in such proportions that nourishment can be extracted and a sufficient amount of bulk provided to maintain body temperature, satisfy the appetite, and produce the required work without digestive disturbance or loss of weight. No one food will accomplish this, therefore the amounts should be properly balanced.

AMOUNT OF FOOD—The amount of food varies greatly, being regulated largely by the size of the animal, work required, and temperature. It is easily understood that other things being equal, a small individual will require less food for maintenance than a larger one; the horse at hard work will need more energy than one at rest; and in severe, cold weather more heat-producing food is required than during warm weather. Sudden changes in either the kind of food or the amount may cause indigestion or colic. Horses accustomed to hard work and large amounts of food need attention when given a rest period. Feed may be reduced about half on such occasions. Many like to give a bran mash on Saturday night when the horse is to rest Sunday, and give a reduced amount of feed the following day. This is done to prevent azoturia (Monday morning disease) which usually occurs in nightly fed animals accustomed to regular work. It often follows a rest period and appears when the animal starts to work. The attack is sudden, the horse being excited and acting as if badly injured in the back or hind legs. There is marked pain, rapid breathing and profuse sweating. The urine is coffee-colored and frequently retained.

KIND OF FEED — 1. Oats. Experience has shown that oats are the best grain for horsefeeding. It supplies considerable nourishment, some bulk, and most horses like them. 2. Corn. Corn is less desirable than oats because of its tendency to produce fat. It is useful in very cold climates and for fattening. It may be mixed with oats and legume hay to provide a satisfactory ration. 3. Barley. Barley is a good grain for horses and may be substituted for oats. Because it is so hard it is usually soaked or crushed before feeding. 4. Bran. Bran is an excellent food for horses, especially since it has a mild laxative effect. It helps in bone and muscle building and is not fattening. The practice of giving a bran mash once a week or so at regular intervals is often helpful. 5. Salt. Salt is essential, especially in certain areas where the water and crops are abnormally low in salt content. 6. Legume hay. This is an excellent food, however care must be exercised to avoid large amounts. It is laxative and produces large amounts of urine, and may injure the kidneys. If mixed with timothy, grass or grain hay it may be used to good advantage. 7. Hay. Hay provides most of the bulk of the ration and cannot be entirely dispensed with unless straw or a similar food is provided. Timothy, oat, and prairie hay are best suited for horse-feeding. 8. Grazing. This is very beneficial because of the laxative value and the stimulating effect upon the appetite. Care must be taken to avoid overeating when they are first turned out or colic may result. Green pasture may replace the feeding of bran.

PRINCIPLES OF FEEDING—The stomach of the horse is small, having a capacity of about two to four gallons depending upon the size of the horse. The large intestine has great capacity and most of the food is stored in this part of the digestive tract. Water passes directly through the stomach and small intestine. If the ear is placed against the side of the animal while it is drinking the rushing of the water can be heard. This has been the reason for the practice of watering before feeding, since if the stomach contained recently chewed food the water passing through would carry a considerable portion of it directly to the large intestine before the digestive juices of the stomach and small intestine complete their function of splitting the food constituents so that they may be absorbed. As a result much of this food would pass through the animal without supplying the full amount of nourishment and perhaps cause colic. Water taken an hour after feeding does not carry as much food as if given immediately, and if watered before feeding the animal will usually drink only a small amount following the meal. The horse will enjoy the food more if the thirst has been quenched before eating a dry meal. Due to the small size of the stomach it is best when possible to feed often and in small amounts. Thus animals at hard labor should be given most of the bulk (hay or grass) at night to avoid working with a full stomach. Often it is not convenient but it would be desirable to feed the grain after the hay to allow more complete digestion. The following rules may be helpful:

1. All food should be of good quality.
2. Water before feeding.
3. Feeding should be done regularly and in regular amounts.
4. The amount of food depends largely upon the size of the horse and the kind of work it is doing.

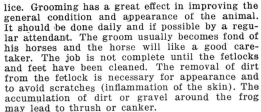

GROOMING — The objects of grooming are cleanliness, prevention of disease and improvement in appearance. An animal at work and left ungroomed will soon develop an accumulation of sweat, dirt, and dandruff in the hair. If this is not removed it may lead to an inflamation of skin or forms an excellent condition for mange or lice. Grooming has a great effect in improving the general condition and appearance of the animal. It should be done daily and if possible by a regular attendant. The groom usually becomes fond of his horses and the horse will like a good caretaker. The job is not complete until the fetlocks and feet have been cleaned. The removal of dirt from the fetlock is necessary for appearance and to avoid scratches (inflammation of the skin). The accumulation of dirt or gravel around the frog may lead to thrush or canker.

CARE OF THE FEET—The old saying, "the horse is as old as his feet" and "no foot—no horse" are even more true today than in the past because so many horses live under unnatural conditions such as standing in stables much of the time or being worked upon paved streets. The wild horse living on the plains, traveling, resting and eating at will, was free from many complications that domesticated horses must endure. Modern use of horses is such that care of the feet is very important.

Growth of the Hoof—The horny parts of the hoof consist of the wall, sole, frog, and bars. These parts have no blood or nerve supply and receive nourishment from the deeper sensitive structures. The wall grows from the top (hair line), the so-called coronary band. The wall of the normal hoof grows about one-fourth of an inch per month. The horny sole grows from the underlying sensitive sole. As it gets old it cracks and flakes, peels or wears off. The frog is the elastic wedge-shaped part between the bars and sole. The bars are extensions of the wall from the heel to the frog. The purpose of these parts is to protect the sensitive structures and absorb shock when the foot strikes the ground.

Trimming the Feet—Ordinarily, colts allowed sufficient pasture room for normal exercise will wear the hoof gradually so that it is only necessary to rasp down the sharp edges of the toe in order to prevent breaking of the wall. Those confined to stables will need more attention. As the horse matures, trimming varies depending upon the work and the surface which the animal travels upon.

The tools needed are the rasp, hoof-cutter and hoof-knife. First, raise the foot and with the hoof-knife remove the flaky over-growth of sole but under no circumstances should any of the solid sole be taken away. Then with the hoof-cutter remove the wall until it is about even with the trimmed sole which will usually give a heel and toe of proper length. With the rasp, smooth the flat surface and sharp corners. The outer surface of the hoof wall should not be touched with the rasp because if the waxy surface is removed, evaporation may take place to such an extent that the wall becomes hard, brittle, and less elastic than normal. The bars strengthen the heel and should not be reduced when trimming the hoof.

SHOEING—The work done by many horses is such that shoeing is necessary. Shoes should be reset every 6 weeks to compensate for normal growth.

DING SKIRTS

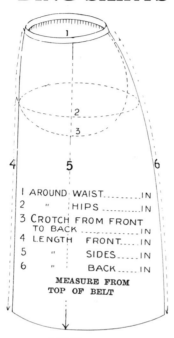

1 AROUND WAIST..........IN
2   "   HIPS ....IN
3 CROTCH FROM FRONT
   TO BACK ....IN
4 LENGTH FRONT....IN
5   "   SIDES.....IN
6   "   BACK.....IN

MEASURE FROM
TOP OF BELT

— — HOW TO MEASURE — —
SEND FOR ORDER BLANKS

SKIRTS MADE ANY SPECIAL STYLE OR
OF MATERIAL TO FIT YOUR REQUIRE-
MENTS — EXTRA LARGE SIZES COST
MORE
ALL SKIRTS ARE SILK SEWED

A handsome garment. Novel two-tone effect; golden brown leather with dark brown trimmings. Solid nickel conchas and buttons, all double sewed with silk. Made to measure.

Also made in combinations of light and dark brown, pearl smoked, black or white.

No. 10

Extra heavy fine sheep; soft glove tan, velvet finish or smooth side out as desired. Price................$26.00

No. 15

No. 1 quality horsehide, velvet finish only.
Price $30.00

Either of above less the nickel trimmings.
Deduct $3.75

A plain serviceable article with all seams double sewed with silk and made to measure.

No. 25

Fine heavy sheep, soft and tough; light or dark brown, pearl or black. Velvet or smooth side out as preferred.
Double fringe on bottom, all silk sewed............$18.00
Extra fringe on bottom and pockets, all silk sewed.... 2.50

No. 30

Fine buffed horse hide, golden brown, velvet finish.
Price $23.50

Solid nickel buttons on side and bottom seams, pockets and belt, extra...............................$2.50

No. 35—Fine soft calfskin, smooth side out........$25.00

No. 40

Extra quality corduroy. Brown or other colors.
No fringe....................................$13.50

This corduroy is the finest and most durable made, and not to be compared to the flimsy stuff often put into skirts.

Flower stamp belts extra $2.50
ANY CHANGES DESIRED WILL BE MADE.

THESE PRICES ARE FOR ORDINARY SIZE SKIRTS—EXTRA LARGE SKIRTS WILL COST EXTRA

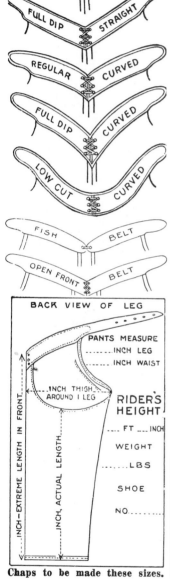

Chaps to be made these sizes.

DIRECTIONS FOR ORDERING CHAPS

Give your height, weight, size shoe, waist measure, length of inseam, thigh measure (one leg), and be sure to state if measures sent are pants or overall measures, or the sizes you want the Chaps made. Please bear in mind that our Chaps actually measure the length they are sold for and not an inch or two short, as is usually the case. If you order a 30 or 31 leg Chap, for instance, they will actually measure that length. Most riders order Chaps too long: for that reason, please be particular to send correct measurements. Please state if a snug fit is wanted or large legs to accommodate overshoes. **25 per cent deposit required on C. O. D. Express or Parcel Post orders.**

CHANGES

Half lined, 50 cents less than full lined. Full lined, add 50 cents to price of half lined. Full lined with glove leather, $3.50. Half lined with glove leather, $2.50. Leather facing to take wear of stirrups, 75 cents. Basket stamped belts 50 cents less than flower stamped. Conchas on belt, $1.00.

All Chaps over 30 actual leg measurement charged extra 25 cents per inch.

NO. 1
CALIFORNIA
CUT LEG

5 SNAPS
AND RINGS

NO. 2
TEXAS
CUT LEG

4 SNAPS
AND RINGS

NO. 3
CHEYENNE
CUT LEG

3 SNAPS
AND RINGS

ALL CHAPS WILL BE MADE TEXAS CUT UNLESS OTHERWISE SPECIFIED

PACKAGES CAN BE SENT C. O. D. BY PARCEL POST ONLY TO MONEY ORDER OFFICES.
IF NOT A MONEY ORDER OFFICE, REMITTANCE IN FULL, INCLUDING POSTAGE, MUST
ACCOMPANY THE ORDER.
BE SURE TO SEND ENOUGH POSTAGE, WE RETURN WHAT IS NOT USED. INSUFFICIENT POSTAGE CAUSES DELAY IN SHIPPING.

ARMITAS

No. 25

No. 20—Our best oil tan chap leather or soft glove leather, brown or drab All buck sewed by hand.
.... $16.00

No. 21—Same as above, only heavy thread sewed.
.... $15.00

No. 22—Plain belt. No pockets $14.00

No. 25—No side stays. Our best buffed glove leather. Heavy thread sewed $12.00

No. 26—Heavy oak tan russet goat skin $8.00

A very useful article for summer wear

FINE WING CHAPS
Examine 'em Carefully

No. 1416..**$110.00**

The round wing pattern is admired by many, so we show a new one here. This is an extra fine piece of work. Genuine California oiltan calfskin, with layers of dark chocolate; extra fine sterling silver conchas and buckle.

No. 1418..**$36.50**

Same as No. 1416 with solid nickle trimmings.

No. 1420..**$33.00**

Same pattern as No. 1416, but legs and trimmings all of oak oiltan chap leather, or any combination of chocolate brown or chocolate; solid nickle ornaments.

No. 1400..**$33.50**

An entirely new and striking design. Made of chocolate chap leather, with pearl trimmings, hearts and large diamonds red inset, with smaller diamonds chocolate inset, with solid nickle ornaments.

One of the showiest chaps we have ever made, and one that will give you plenty of service; also made with any combination of brown oak oiltan leather, black, chocolate and pearl. Same price.

"Walker" Chaps "oh Boy"

TWO DELUX DESIGNS—A CLASS BY THEMSELVES

No. 1928—Sterling silver trimmed $90.00
1928-P—Nickle trimmed 55.00

No. 1929—Sterling silver trimmed $87.50
1929-P—Without silver 57.50

Finest grade of pearl glove leather with genuine calfskin facings and trimmings.

Genuine California oak tan calfskin; finest
quality.

Both numbers have the background of the stamping blackened,
giving a very striking and handsome effect to the trimmings.

**WE MAKE A SPECIALTY OF FINE SILVER MOUNTED GOODS FOR THE RODEO AND SHOW TRADE
IF YOU WANT SOMETHING DIFFERENT OR OUT OF THE ORDINARY, WRITE US.**

"Walker" Chaps-Wear

LEATHER WING CHAPS

SNAPS AND RINGS AT SIDES

No. 1390—$28.75   No. 1360—$25.50   No. 222—$23.50   No. 1370—$29.25

ALL SEAMS HAND BUCK SEWED

These Chaps are made of our genuine oak bark, California tanned stock; tough, soft; durable, and will turn the water. Made usually medium heft, but will be sent either light or heavy for those who prefer them, if so ordered. Also made of soft glove leather if preferred, drab or brown. Made flesh side out if preferred.

All the conchas and buttons used are solid nickel, which will not wear brassy. They cost much more than the common nickel plated stuff so generally used, and which soon turns brassy after the plating wears off.

WE MAKE ANY SPECIAL STYLE YOU PREFER

Walker Chaps all California Leather

LEATHER WING CHAPS, SNAPS AND RINGS

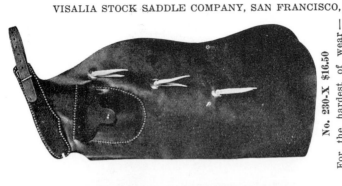

No. 230-X $16.50

For the hardest of wear — Chrome leather buck sewed by hand.

Nickle conchas and Texas cut.

No. 225—$21.00

No. 1 stock and all buck sewed by hand. All hand copper riveted.

Any leather chaps waterproofed extra $1.00

RUGGED CHAPS FOR RANGE USE

LEATHER CHAPS, CLOSED LEGS

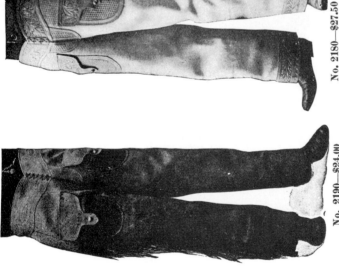

No. 2190—$24.00

Plain. Concealed lacings down the side. Buck sewed, $2.50 extra.

No. 2191—$23.00

Made with sewed side seams in place of lacing.

No. 2180—$27.50
Flower Stamp

No. 2182—$25.00
Basket Stamp

Nickel buttons and concealed lacing down the sides. Less buttons, deduct 50c. Buck sewed, $2.50 extra.

Closed leg chaps made of No. 1 Genuine California Oak tanned calf skin, the toughest made, $2.50 extra.

These chaps are made of genuine oak bark, oil-tanned stock, soft, durable, and will turn water. Made usually medium heft. Made of soft glove leather if preferred, if so ordered. Also made of soft glove leather if preferred, but will be sent either light or heavy for those who prefer them. Extra heavy stock, extra $1.50, for thorns and cactus. drab or brown.

ANY SPECIAL CHAPS MADE TO ORDER

WING CHAPS

Some More New Designs — Look 'em Over

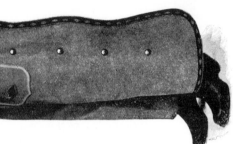

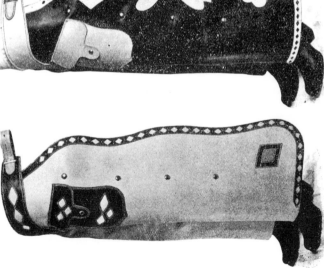

No. 1402......$26.50
Pearl chap legs and chocolate trimmings.

No. 1404......$24.50
Chocolate chap legs, pearl trimmings.

Also made from our California oak oiltan chap leather with contrasting trimmings or any combination of oak oiltan, chocolate, pearl or black you may desire. Small diamonds are inset with nickle spots between, large diamonds red patent leather, snaps and rings at back; any style leg.

No. 1150......$17.50   No. 1175......$14.50

Chocolate trimmings, heavy olive chrome buff leather. Soft, pliable, and tough as "all get-out." They sure wear. The finest brush chap made at these prices.

Where a fellow doesn't want to put out a lot of money in chaps these will fill the bill, and surprise him. Try 'em and they won't disappoint you as to wear or looks.

Walker Chaps all California Leather

BEST IN THE WEST
SINCE 1870

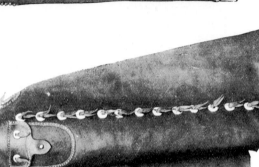

No. 3250—Price $44.50

Made in Brown or Chocolate Glove Leather with Pearl Trimmings—Solid Nickle Ornaments—Flower-stamped Belt

No. 1375X—Price $29.50

Our Best Oak-Tan Leather, all Buck Sewed—Solid Nickle Trimmings — Flower-stamped Belt.

No. 3100—Price $45.00

Made in Brown or Chocolate Glove Leather with Pearl Trimmings, Metal Trimmings, Solid Nickle

"Walker" since 1870

EXTRA FINE ANGORA CHAPS

WITH WINGS   **CLOSED LEGS**

No. 350—Spotted...$35.50
No. 351—No spots...$33.50

Wings extra heavy canvas lined. Full canvas lined. Also made Black, Lemon, Orange, Gold or Red. Snaps and Rings at sides.

No. 122—White, as illustrated....................$30.50
No. 125—Black spots, conchas on belt........$32.00
Also made Black, Gold, Orange, Lemon or Red.

You can have any combination of colors for the fronts and spots—white, black, orange, lemon, gold or red. Made of our finest skins, full-lined with the very best double filled canvas, leather pockets, buck sewed bindings, and fine flower-stamped belts.

WE ORIGINATED SPOTTED CHAPS IN 1911

"Walker" Chaps-Wear
FINE ANGORA CHAPS—CLOSED LEGS

No. 160—$28.50
Fine long fur.

No. 150—Medium Fur...$27.00
No. 140—Short Fur......$26.25

Full canvas lined. Flower belts.
Our Best Grade Genuine Oak Bark Tanned Skins.
Black, Gold, Orange, Lemon or Red.

No. 130—Long Fur.......$26.25
No. 135—Medium Fur...$25.00
Made with concealed leather cuffs at bottom, flower belt, half canvas lined.

No. 165—White........$28.50
Selected long fur. Best chrome tan drab glove backs.
No. 155—White........$27.50
Same as above, but with medium length fur.

These chaps are made up with great care of our very best materials, best grade double filledcanvas linings, all seams sewed with extra-heavy waxed linen thread, and all bindings buck sewed by hand. They are a thoroughly dependable line of goods, and are giving splendid service to thousands of satisfied users, and you make no mistake in trying them. THE BEST AND MOST DURABLE CHAPS ON THE MARKET TODAY. Many riders have had a costly experience with chaps made with alum tanned fur fronts. Long exposure has proved to us that the combination of alum tan and dye in fur skins affects the life of the skin, causing it to rot in time from the exposure to the elements. We have also proven that the only tannage that will stand the test of time and hard service, is the genuine oak bark tannage. We use this exclusively in all our chaps, which accounts for the long service whichthey give to the wearer. TRY 'EM. For those who are obliged to ride in extremely wet weather we line our chaps with extra-heavy water proof canvas; full lined $1.00 extra; half lined 50c extra

"BUTTERFLY"

Owned by
Mrs.
Vern Nidever
of
Carpenteria,
Calif.

Showing
silver mounted
Saddle, Bridle
and Martingale
Made by
VISALIA STOCK
SADDLE CO.

pirited, gentle, intelligent. Sired by "Swedish King." A half-sister of Mr. Dwight Murphy's famous alomino stallion, but is more golden than Palomino. Naturally gaited with seven gaits instead of the usual five. Has been ridden twice from the coast to the top of the U. S., 800 miles, and 50 miles a day is no task for her.

Visalia Stock Saddle Company excels again in silver mounted riding equipment! We have made the utfits for many of the finest horses to be found in the United States.

We have our own designer and silversmith and are equipped to make up, to your order, an outfit incorporating any special designs of silver trimmings that might appeal to you. Send us a rough sketch of what you have in mind, and we will work it up and quote approximate price.

JUSTIN BOOTS
THE VISALIA SPECIAL

This handsome Boot was designed by us and made by H. J. Justin & Sons, Manufacturers of the Celebrated Cowboy Boots. This number is in keeping with the Visalia Saddles that have given such wonderful satisfaction to the Western Man wherever the occasion has demanded a saddle of unusual stamina.

The Visalia Special has a Black Australian Kangaroo Vamp, is lined with a soft, smooth leather that makes the foot feel comfortable from the first minute it is slipped into the boot. The top is a beautiful glossy Black Morocco Kid inlaid with a White Butterfly. The wing dots of the butterfly are red making the design most daring and attractive. The height is the popular 13 inch, the heel is correctly set for riding purposes, while the arch is made of steel and re-inforced with two rows of pegs thus making it perfectly rigid.

In this selection of boots the Visalia Stock Saddle Company knows the numbers listed in this catalog can be recommended without hesitancy. You cannot go astray by ordering from us as we are in a position to give you service and the best types of boots in the latest designs.

When Justin

Makes 'em You

Know They're

Right!

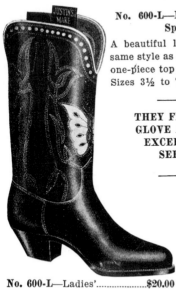

No. 600-L—Ladies' Visalia Special

A beautiful lightweight boot same style as **No. 600** but with one-piece top and back seam. Sizes 3½ to 7. Price....**$22.50**

THEY FIT LIKE A GLOVE AND GIVE EXCEPTIONAL SERVICE

Men's sizes 5½ to 10½ Don't forget yours!

Made-to-measure Boots $2.00 extra.

When full amount is sent with order we pay postage.

No. 600-L—Ladies'..................$20.00

No. 600—Men's.....................................$22.00

JUSTIN BOOTS

NEW PRICES!

Nos. 650-RC and 650-C

No. 650-RC BLACK LIGHT FRENCH CALF
A splendid new boot with 1¾ full undershot heels, Steel heel plates 14-inch one-piece tops, combination D width last—
$25.00

We should call these boots "Black Prince." Black kid top with four rows of silk stitching that make this boot look exceedingly rich. White dotted diamonds and piping are around the top.

Sizes 5½ to 10½

BE SURE TO STATE YOUR SIZE

Boots delivered free if full amount is sent

640—Tan, square toes.

THE ARISTOCRAT

Kid top, tan calf vamps, with four rows of silk stitching as illustrated. White diamonds inlaid at the top, also white piping. You'll be very pleased with this quality boot. Height 12 inches.

PRICE..............................$21.00

Notice the toe
It is a medium narrow, square box toe.

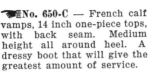

No. 650-C — French calf vamps, 14 inch one-piece tops, with back seam. Medium height all around heel. A dressy boot that will give the greatest amount of service.

No. 650-C—French calf....$22.50

No. 640

Tan Calf—Round Toe
No. 640-J—Ladies' Boots
Same style at 640 but with one piece top and back seam. Round toe. This elegant and light weight boot is sure to please—It never fails! Sizes 3½ to 7. 14-inch tops.
Tan Leather.....................$21.00

Made to Measure Boots—$2.00 Extra

JUSTIN BOOTS

NEW PRICES!
THEY STAMPEDE
for these "THREE ACES"

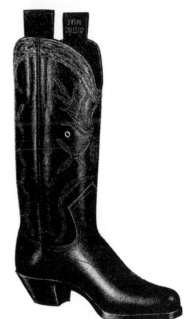

No. 615 (above)

The Ace of Diamonds!

Black Cereco Vamp (California tanned) Toe stitched as illustrated, top of black kid with one row of ornamental stitching. This is the JUSTIN that not only gives super service but looks neat and trim and is fit for any occasion. The height is 13 inches. PRICE $17.00

Sizes 5½ to 10½

BE SURE TO STATE YOUR SIZE

No. 625 (below)

The Ace of Hearts:

Because it appeals to your heart due to its comfort. Soft Black Kangaroo Vamp, Black Kid top, stitched toe, soft lined vamp, 14 inches, one piece. PRICE............$22.00

No. 621 (above)
The Ace of Spades:

Genuine French calf vamps, black Kid tops with three rows of stitching, used by JUSTIN'S for years without a single complaint as to its wear. This is a fine boot that wears and wears, and wears. Height is 14 inches.
PRICE $22.00

Made to Measure Boots $2.00 Extra

No. 625

WE DELIVER FREE WHEN FULL AMOUNT IS SENT WITH ORDER

JUSTIN BOOTS

NEW PRICES

V-3638

This is one of our special designs of dress boot from the famous House of Justin. Specially selected tan Russian calf vamps, lined with soft kid. Brown glossy kid tops with four rows of blue and yellow stitching. Attractive white underlay pattern, with white beading around the top. One-piece tops, round toe, 13 inches high. A, B and D widths, sizes 6 to 12. **Price $23.50**

No. 326-J—Black....
A new, handsome pattern, soft Elk vamps and 13½ in. kid tops with white tulips inlaid. Sizes 1 to 7 only.
PRICE...........**$14.75**

LONGHORN BRAND

We prepay postage if full amount is sent with order

No. V-3638

A JUSTIN creation designed to meet the demand of the trade that does not feel the need of higher priced boots. Black Elk Vamp and Black Kid top. A wonderful value for its cost. Height is 12 inches. **Price $13.50**

Every lad has been anxious for a pair of boots like Dad and the REGULARS wear. Here we are, black elk vamp, black kid top, inlay work is of white kid. Sizes 10 to 2— little boys. 10 inch height, No. 654 ....$10.75

No. 655
Youth's sizes 2½ to 7....**$11.75**
BOTH WITH ONE-PIECE TOPS

Made to Measure Boots—$2.00 extra

DON'T FORGET YOUR SIZE—IT SAVES DELAY TO MENTION IT WHEN ORDERING
Sizes 5½ to 10½
Nos. 654, 655

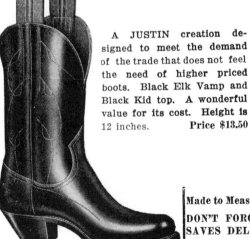

No. 645

No. 654 - 655

Fine Imported English Boots

FIELD
BOOTS
No. 825
Men's
$25.00

QUALITY HIGH — PRICES LOW

POSTAGE PAID WHEN FULL AMOUNT IS SENT

Same description as No. 800, but with short lacing at instep. Fine imported, genuine calf.

An extra fine boot, built for hard service.

A high-grade imported boot at a moderate price, built especially for us by one of the foremost bootmakers of England.

Calf Lined

ENGLISH STYLE JODPHUR SHOES Made of the finest Freidenberg tanned calf. In russet color only. Made on the elastic gaiter style which eliminates the bundlesome ankle straps.

Ladies' sizes only 3½ to 7½
C Widths only—Price....$8.00

No. 825—$25.00

800

No. 800—Men's............$25.00

Finest grade imported English riding boots, welted tongues, stiff legs, 18 ins. high, with bevel tops, back-seams. All genuine calf.

No. 820—LADIES' TAN......$24.00
Same as 800—16½ in. leg.

No. 851—LADIES' BLACK..$22.50
Same as 820

We are all aware of the wonderful wearing qualities of English tanned leather, and as to workmanship there's none finer.

Fine oak-tan calf vamps and one-piece back-seam tops.

No. 801—Men's, 6 to 11..........$18.00
    802—Ladies', 3 to 7½...... 17.50
    10-Y—Youths' sizes 2½
    to 6.................................. 14.75
    10-B—Boys', sizes 12 to
    2 ....$13.75

Ladies — 16-inch tops
Youths — 13-inch tops
Men —— 18-inch tops
Boys —— 12-inch tops
Nos. 801, 802, 10Y, 10B

Delivered free when full amount is sent!

WE MUST KNOW YOUR SIZE. PLEASE MENTION IT!

No. 550

Ladies'

15½ in. tops
$13.50

BE SURE TO SEND YOUR SIZE!

WE'RE MIGHTY POOR GUESSERS

No. 500—Men's $14.50

Tan English Boot. Genuine calf; 16-inch legs, one piece back-seam. Calf vamps; 1-inch heels; very stylish and durable.

BOOTS

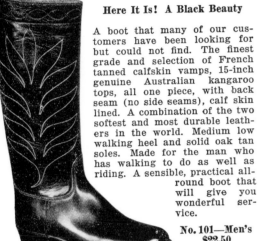

Here It Is! A Black Beauty

A boot that many of our customers have been looking for but could not find. The finest grade and selection of French tanned calfskin vamps, 15-inch genuine Australian kangaroo tops, all one piece, with back seam (no side seams), calf skin lined. A combination of the two softest and most durable leathers in the world. Medium low walking heel and solid oak tan soles. Made for the man who has walking to do as well as riding. A sensible, practical all-round boot that will give you wonderful service.

No. 101—Men's
$22.50

No. 101

LADIES' COMBINATION ENGLISH AND WESTERN BOOT

A beautiful russet leather calf boot, with high heel, and 16-inch English type one-piece top.

This boot combines the English top with the Western high heel, giving the wearer the protection from the foot going through the stirrup.

Semi-stiff tops. Combination last. C width only.

No. 562

Price

$14.00

YOUR SIZE?

A novel and very popular style of ladies' English calf boot. Thirteen-inch top; stiffened; with back seams, calf vamp; 1¼-inch heel, cowboy style. Sizes 3¼ to 8.

OUR NEW POLO BOOT

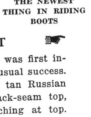

A new creation. A combination of the English top with a modified Western heel. A most comfortable and good-looking boot for riding and walking.

THE NEWEST THING IN RIDING BOOTS

No. 807—POLO BOOT

This new and most practical boot was first introduced by us and has met with unusual success. It is made of a very fine grade of tan Russian calf, with a 14 inch, one-piece back-seam top, with white piping and scroll stitching at top. Best solid oak soles, and heels just the right height for comfort in walking and security in riding.

No. 807 ....**$22.50**

Sizes 6 to 10½

No. 807—Price $22.50

No. 525—Tan—$16.00

No. 561—Same style as **No. 807** boot but for light wear, tan calf vamp and soft kid tops. Ideal for the man or woman who wants a practical and very comfortable boot. Size 3½ to 11. C widths. **Price**...**$14.00**

BOOT SHOES

Cowboy shoes are becoming more popular each day, not only among former wearers of boots but also among policemen, workmen and others on their feet a great deal. The shoe gives absolute arch support, the needed comfort and rest.

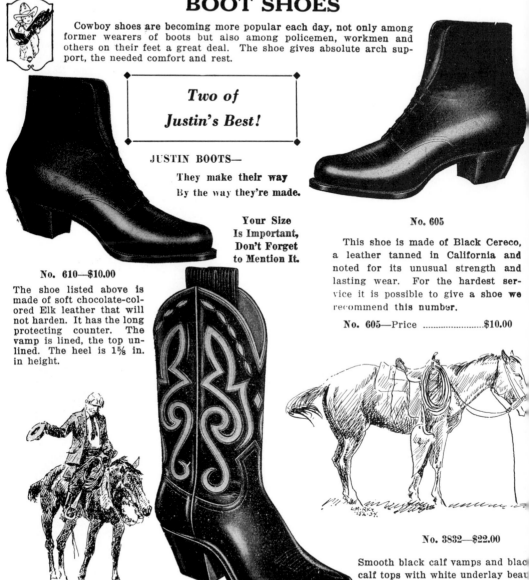

Two of Justin's Best!

JUSTIN BOOTS—

They make their way
By the way they're made.

Your Size Is Important, Don't Forget to Mention It.

No. 610—$10.00

The shoe listed above is made of soft chocolate-colored Elk leather that will not harden. It has the long protecting counter. The vamp is lined, the top unlined. The heel is 1⅝ in. in height.

No. 605

This shoe is made of Black Cereco, a leather tanned in California and noted for its unusual strength and lasting wear. For the hardest service it is possible to give a shoe we recommend this number.

No. 605—Price $10.00

No. 3832—$22.00

Smooth black calf vamps and black calf tops with white underlay beautifully designed — Medium square toe, 12 in. height, 2 in. heel. In stock, E width, sizes 5 to 10.

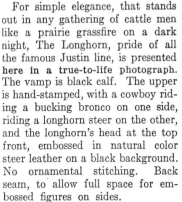

OUR FINEST
THE LAST WORD IN FINE FOOTWEAR

The LONGHORN

For simple elegance, that stands out in any gathering of cattle men like a prairie grassfire on a dark night, The Longhorn, pride of all the famous Justin line, is presented here in a true-to-life photograph. The vamp is black calf. The upper is hand-stamped, with a cowboy riding a bucking bronco on one side, riding a longhorn steer on the other, and the longhorn's head at the top front, embossed in natural color steer leather on a black background. No ornamental stitching. Back seam, to allow full space for embossed figures on sides.

An Unusual Value at
$60.00
Per Pair

MADE TO ORDER ONLY. WRITE US AND BE SURE TO GIVE YOUR SIZE.

These boots combine the art of the leather workers, with the skill of the bootmaker, and the result of the combined efforts of the house of Walker, and the house of Justin, both pioneers in their lines, is the superb boots shown here.

No. 1650 _____$60.00

This Boot, whether in colors or with black background as shown, with the figures true to life, is the "Ne Plus Ultra" of Boots.

We can conceive of no more elegant or refined style of ornamentation for a boot, and we can vary the patterns and designs with initials, monograms and brands as desired.

Made to order only.
Don't forget your size.
We have also ornamented these boots with appropriate silver trimmings.

WRITE US ABOUT THEM!

No. 1600
This number is built of the finest California calf tops, elaborately flower stamped, black background, with genuine calf vamps, any color desired. The designs can be varied with your initials or brand worked in.

No. 1625

Same as No. 1600,
$50.00
without black background

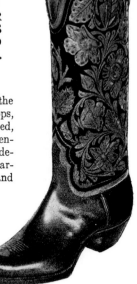

No. 1600 _____$55.00

STARNES BOOTS

"OUT OF THE WEST   COMES THE BEST"

BOYS' COWBOY BOOT

No. 5131-X—Price $6.95

Boy's black chrome, cowboy round-toe last, rider's steel shank. Single sole. Ten-inch tops, 1½ inch cowboy heel. Wide widths, sizes 1 to 6. Has white star in front.

Rugged as the Monarch of the Rockies

BE SURE TO SEND YOUR SIZE

No. 8405

Fine black kip vamp, black kid leg, 12-inch tops, round toe, with two rows of fancy stitching on leg. Hand-made undershot heel, with alternate red and white inlay around top.

No. 8405—$13.00

No. 5134-X—Price $8.95

Boy's black kid vamp, with brown kid leg, single sole. Cowboy round-toe last, rider's steel shank. Leather lined. White star inlaid top. Ten-inch tops, wide width, 1½-inch heels.

SQUARE TOE BOOT SHO[E]

No. 8305—Price $7.75

Here is a shoe detailed to cov[er] everything the rider deman[ds]. Uppers are black chrome elk; he[els] are hand built, underslung to [the] greatest pitch. Note the spur coun[ter] and square toe. Overweight soles. Sizes from 5½ to 11.
No. 6305—As above, black round t[oe].
No. 5305—As above, chocolate rou[nd] toe. Same price.

Low in Price—High in Qual[ity]

"POSTAGE PAID WHEN CASH ACCOMPANIES ORDERS"

STARNES BOOTS

"OUT OF THE WEST COMES THE BEST"

LADIES' COWBOY BOOT

No. 1705 — Price $12.00

A beautiful light-weight boot for the ladies. Uppers are made of fine smooth black calf.

Twelve inches high; heels are 1¾ inches and shanks are strong and sturdy. White piping at top and two rows of fine silk stitching completes an ensemble befitting the ladies who wear them. Sizes from 4 to 8; C width.

No. 0355

MEN'S DRESS BOOT
Square Toe Last
No. 0355—Price $14.50

In all the world no finer boot for dress wear. Extremely light in weight, it has a strong steel rider's shank. Heels are 2 inches high, hand built, and undershot. Uppers are of the finest black smooth grain calf. Twelve inches high, tops are piped in white. Square toe last. Sizes from 5 to 11.

Russet Vamps—Black Tops
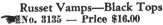
No. 3135 — Price $16.00

A "short top" boot of unusual distinction made to give real hard service and yet dressy to a marked degree. Legs are black kid quilted with fine silk. Vamps are a beautiful shade of russet tan, which we are sure you will like. Square toe last. Two inch heels. Eleven inches high. Sizes from 5½ to 11.

No. 5319

Style No. 5319—Price $16.50

Men's tan calf vamp, with tan kid leg. Single sole. Square toe last. Stitched vamp, heavy steel rider's shank, pegged.; 12-inch tops with 2-inch hand-built underslung heel. Sizes 5 to 11, narrow and wide widths.

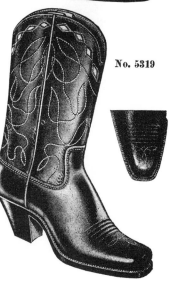

No. 1705

No. 3135

JOHN B. STETSON'S QUALITY

Like That of the D. E. Walker Saddles - - Will Be Long Remembered After the Price is Forgotten

FRONNY 👉

No. 10-S—Price................................$15.00

A large snappy Stetson with a style that only Stetsons have. No. 1 quality, belly color, 7½ in crown, 5-inch brim.

Don't Forget Your Size

FRONNY

Large hats are very much in favor and here two that are great sellers; probably the best in Stetson line.

*   *   *   *   *   *   *   *

👉 TOMMY GRIMES

No. 20-S—Price................................$11.00

No. 1 quality, belly color, 7¼-inch crow 4½-inch brim.

POSTAGE PAID WHEN FULL AMOUNT
SENT WITH ORDER

TOMMY GRIMES

JOHN B. STETSON HATS of QUALITY

THE KINGSTON   POSTPAID WHEN FULL AMOUNT IS SENT   No. 50—Price $15.00

This elegant Stetson dress hat is a feather-weight 3X beaver, silver belly color. The crown is 5½ inches, with brim 2⅛ inches. Has a three-cord band and trimmings, perfectly blended; also white silk linings. You will be proud to wear this hat!

No. 51—Same style and size as No. 50, only in extra quality, buckskin color—Price......................**$10.00**

No. 52—Also same style and size as above—THE KINGWAY — Price......................................**$6.50**

JOHN B. STETSON HATS

THE FINEST IN THE WORLD
ARMINTO

No. 25-S—No. 1 Quality—Price_____$8.

A beautiful brownish buckskin color, wi
cord tobacco colored band and trimmings, 6
crown, 3¼ inch brim.

ST. ARMIN

No. 38-SA—Price_____$12.

Crown, 6 inches; brim, 3 inches; silver belly c
Nutria quality, not lined. This hat has the l
process re-enforced edge, and has no stitchin,
artificial means of holding it together. It adds stre
and lasting beauty to the line of the brim.

AUSTIN

No. 125-S—Price_____$7.50

A splendid and very popular style that never
grows old. No. 1 quality, belly color, size 4½
crown, 3¼ brim.

No. 126—Same style. Chamois Quality—$6.50

THE VISALIA, JR.

No. 50-SL—Price_____$6.

A snappy medium-priced Stetson dress hat

No. 1 quality, size 5¾ crown, 2¾ brim, belly c
Three cord band and narrow bound edge.

John B. Stetson Hats

A SPLENDID DRESS HAT

SAN AN

In real nutria quality, buckskin color, and silk lining, with band and bindings to match, 6¼ inch crown, 3½ inch brim.

No. 5-SN—Buckskin color—Price_____$14.00

No. 6-S—Buck, No. 1 quality—Price____ 8.00

Postage paid when full amount is sent with order

MENTION YOUR SIZE

*   *   *   *

SAN AN,

To those who do not care for a large hat these medium sizes will appeal

SPECIAL ORDERS

For Duplicating Styles Not Shown in Our Catalogue

We can supply any Stetson style, if you write us and send us your old hat, or give us all lot numbers, underneath the sweat band.

*   *   *   *

SAN AN, JR.

No. 1 quality, belly color, 6 inch brim, 3 inch crown.

No. 5-S, Jr.—Price_____$7.00

John B. Stetson's Famous Western Hats

KNOWN THE WIDE WORLD OVER

SAN AN   ☞

One of Stetson's most popular styles.   No. 1
quality, belly color, size 6¼ inch crown, 3½ inch
brim.

No. 5-S—Belly color, No. 1 Quality_____$8.00
No. 6-S—Buck, No. 1 Quality_____ 8.00

SAN AN

CARLSBAD

NOTICE

In ordering be sure to state size of hat wanted.

☞   STETSON'S CARLSBAD

A great favorite with the cowboys.   No. 1 quality, belly color, 7 inch crown, 4 inch brim.

No. 15-S—Price_____$9.50

POSTAGE PAID WHEN FULL AMOUNT IS SENT WITH ORDER

Some Popular Black Stetsons

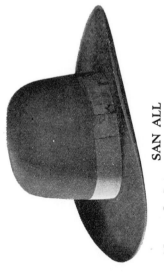

SAN ALL

No. 31-S—Price _____ $9.00

No. 1 quality, 6¾-inch crown, 4-inch brim, silk band and binding.

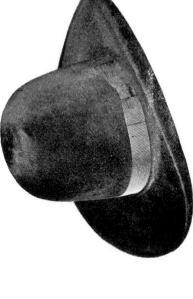

CARLSBAD VELOUR

No. 108-SN—Price _____ $17.50

Nutria quality, silk lined, 7-inch crown, 4-inch brim, silk band and raw edge.

THE CHEUNNEY

No. 36-S—Price _____ $11.00

Crown 7 inches; brim 4½ inches; No. 1 quality, not lined; has a six-cord black band and binding. (See cut on page 85.)

THE "D. E. WALKER"

No. 110-S—Price _____ $7.50

No. 1 quality, silk lined, 5¾-inch crown, 2⅞-inch brim, raw edge, silk cord band.

A FEW NOBBY NEW STETSONS

THE SAN FRAN

6¼-inch crown, 3½-inch brim, 3 cord silk band and binding. We carry them in two grades

No. 100-SN—Buckskin, real Nutria, silk lined......$14.00
No. 102-S—Buckskin, No. 1 quality, not lined..... 8.00

THE SAN FRAN, JR.

6-inch crown, 3-inch brim, 3 cord silk band and binding. In stock in three grades.

No. 105-SN—Buckskin, real Nutria, silk lined....$13.00
No. 106-S—light pearl, No. 1 quality, not lined.... 7.00
No. 107-S—Buckskin, No. 1 quality, not lined...... 7.00

SAN ALL SPECIAL

No. 30-SN—Price..$16.00
Real Nutria quality, buckskin color, size 6¼-inch crown, 4-inch brim. This hat has real style. So don't overlook it, cowboy.

WE PAY POSTAGE when cash is sent with the order

SAN FRAN

No. 101-SW—Price..$8.50
No. 1 quality, pure white, 6¼-inch crown, 3½-inch brim. Lined.

No. 32-BS—Price....$8.00
SAN FRAN—BLACK—No. 1 quality; 6¼-inch crown; 3½ inch brim. Not lined.

THE VISALIA, No. 35-SV

This beautiful Stetson, made exclusively for us, is extremely good looking; has a six-cord band and trimmings delicately blended; is silver belly color, and silk lined; crown 6¼ inches, brim 3½ inches.

Price—$15.00

THE CHEUNNEY—No. 36-S

A BLACK BEAUTY—No. 1 QUALITY

Crown 7 inches; brim 4½ inches; not lined, **and** with a six-cord black band and trimming.

Price—$11.00

HOW TO MEASURE A HAT WHERE THE SIZE IS IN DOUBT

If your head measure is not exactly the size shown on the chart, order next size larger. For example, if your head measures 21¾ or 21⅞ inches, order hat size 7⅛.

Head Measure		Hat Wanted	Head Measure		Hat Wanted	
18⅝ inches		Size 6	21⅝ inches		Size 7	
19	"	" 6⅛	22	"	" 7⅛	
19⅜	"	" 6¼	22⅜	"	" 7¼	
19¾	"	" 6⅜	22¾	"	" 7⅜	
20⅛	"	" 6½	23⅛	"	" 7½	
20½	"	" 6⅝	23½	"	" 7⅝	
20⅞	"	" 6¾	23⅞	"	" 7¾	
21¼	"	" 6⅞	24	"	" 7⅞	

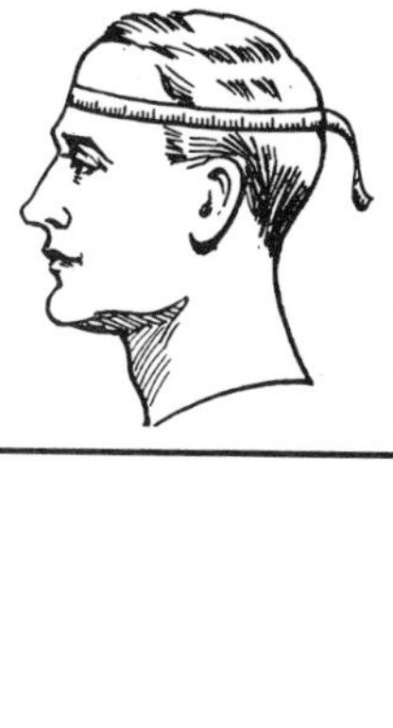

THE VISALIA HUMANE BIT

ACTUAL USE WILL PROVE ITS WORTH

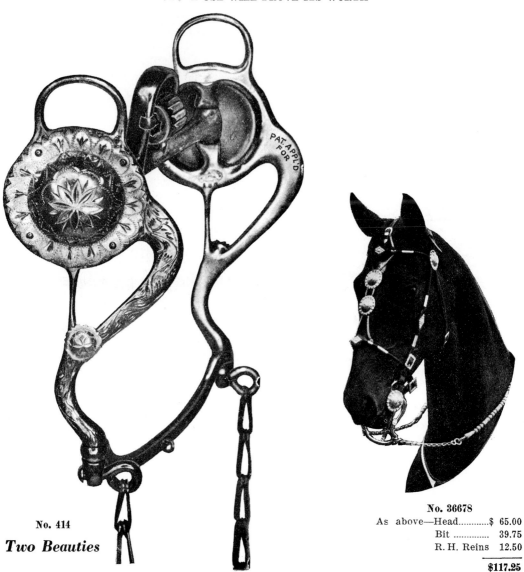

No. 414

Two Beauties

No. 36678
As above—Head............$ 65.00
Bit 39.75
R. H. Reins   12.50

$117.25

—SEE PAGE 87 FOR PRICES—

THE NEW VISALIA HUMANE BIT IS HERE
Proving Its Worth in Everyday Use

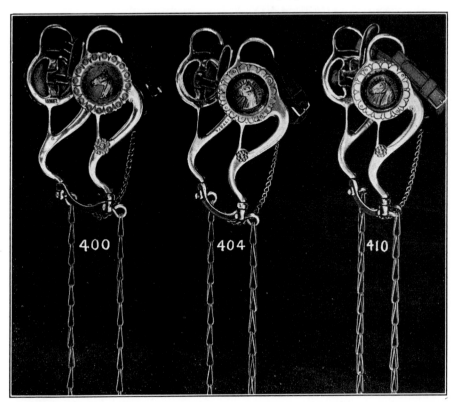

No. 400 Bit—hand made of Monel metal, with 2½ inch No. 100 silver conchas with 14K gold horse heads. Price......$39.75

No. 402 Bit as above, but with silver horse heads. Price..$31.50

No. 414—A beautiful hand-made Monel Bit with 2½ inch sterling silver conchas and the Monel sides of Bit beautifully engraved. Price ....$31.50 If wanted with spoon spade $3.00 extra.

No. 404 Bit—Monel metal with 2½ inch No. 130 sterling silver conchas, with large gold bronc or horse head. Price.....$37.25

No. 406 Bit—as above, but with large raised silver horse heads. Price $29.00

No. 408 Bit—as above, with engraved star instead of horse heard. Price..........$29.00

No. 410 Bit—Monel metal, with conchas also of Monel, spoon spade, slightly tilted back. Price $28.00

No. 411—As above, less spoon spade. Price............$25.00

No. 412 Bit — as above, with gold-colored metal horse heads. Price $29.50

Any of above Bits engraved as No. 414 on page 86 Price ....$2.50 extra Any of above Bits less spoon spade deduct $3.00

We can furnish any of the bits listed above in white rustless steel for $2.50 less than quoted for the monel metal.

NOTE: We prepay the postage on hats, boots, bits and spurs when the full amount of the purchase price accompanies the order. For postage on other goods, consult the parcels post chart.

VISALIA HUMANE
STOCKMEN'S AND
POLO BITS

*See pages 86-87-89
for Prices*

RIDGEWOOD RANCH
C. S. HOWARD

REGISTERED HEREFORDS

TRIANGLE-H
H
BRAND

| SAN FRANCISCO OFFICE 1601 VAN NESS AVENUE | WILLITS, MENDOCINO CO., CAL. | TELEPHONE RIDGEWOOD RANCH VIA UKIAH |

Jan 4th, 1934

Visalia Stock Saddle Co.,
2117 Market St.,
San Francisco, Calif.
    Attention Mr. Lee Bergen

Dear Lee:

    Am sending my bit under separate cover to
have the "kinks" taken out. Please get it back to
me as soon as possible, as I am spoiled for using
any other bit.

    Must be good stuff in this bit and easy on
a horse--when a 1250 lb. horse running down hill can
stand on his head and only bend the bit and not hurt
his mouth except for a very small cut on his tongue.

    With kindest regards, and a Happy New Year.
I am

        Very truly Yours,

        E E Jofford

**Showing Dr. T. B. Ricks young stock horse
using the Visalia Humane Polo Bit.**

San Francisco, Calif.
February 14, 1935.

Visalia Stock Saddle Co.,
2123 Market St.,
San Francisco, Calif.

Gentlemen:

    I have used the Visalia Humane Polo Bit on
young ponies, and have found it very satisfactory.

        Very truly yours,

        Geo. A. Pope

**In the center, Mr. George A. Pope Jr.'s horse
in action using the Visalia Humane Polo Bit.**

RANCH ‡ BRAND

WILLITS
MENDOCINO CO.,
CALIFORNIA

EDEN VALLEY RANCH
HENSHAW INVESTMENT CO.

REGISTERED HEREFORDS

February 15th, 1935

Visalia Stock Saddle Co.,
2117 Market St.,
San Francisco, Calif.
    Attention Mr. Lee Bergen.

Gentlemen:--

    I wish to commend you on your Humane Polo Bit. For
young hackamore horses going into the bit with two reins it is the
best I have used. You have the effect of the snaffle with the mild curb
which can be used on the most sensitive mouth. The necessary leverage
is there also if needed.

    I particularly like the way the cricket is placed, and with
these features along with its light weight make it ideal for starting
young horses, as well as for general use.

        Yours very truly

        T. B. Ricks

ANOTHER POPULAR

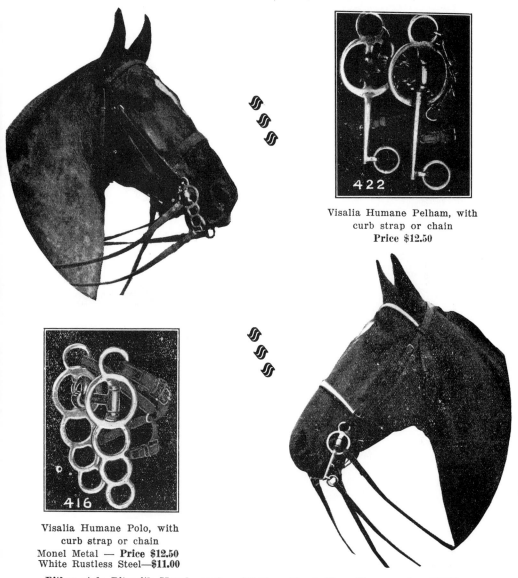

Visalia Humane Pelham, with
curb strap or chain
Price $12.50

Visalia Humane Polo, with
curb strap or chain
Monel Metal — **Price $12.50**
White Rustless Steel—**$11.00**

**Either style Bit with Monel conchas $15.50; with sterling silver conchas $20.00
Monel swivel chains, extra $4.00**

ese Humane Bits are made of Monel metal which is rustless and extremely strong and durable.

FINE SILVER MOUNTED HAND-FORGED BITS

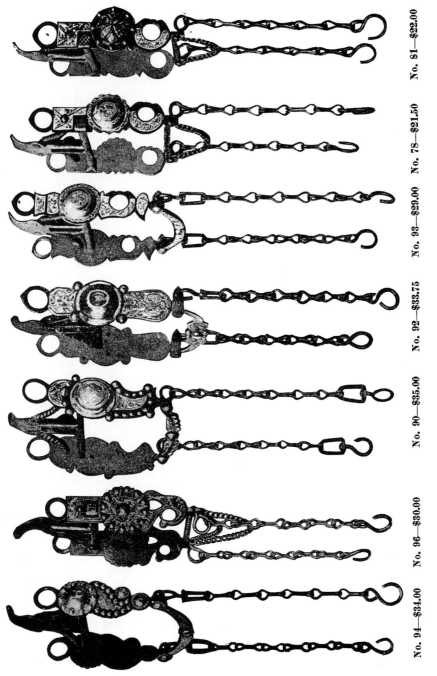

No. 94—$34.00 No. 96—$30.00 No. 90—$35.00 No. 92—$33.75 No. 93—$29.00 No. 78—$21.50 No. 81—$22.00

All our work is inlaid with heavy, pure refined silver. No "dobies" used. We could save 30 per cent of our silver by using Mexican dollars, but we don't. They're not good enough for our work.

EXTRA FINE HAND-MADE BITS
Pure, Refined, Genuine Silver Overlaid

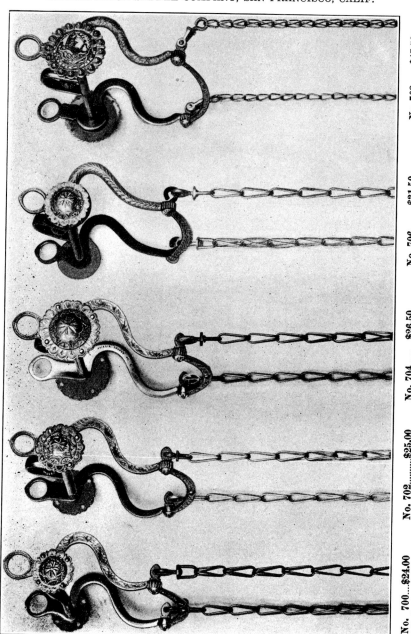

No. 700...$24.00
1¾ inch concha

These are some of the finest pieces of work our shops turn out; light, strong, of the best steel, and overlaid with the finest silver, artistically engraved. They are in a class by themselves. All equipped with hand-made, rust-proof chains.

No. 702......$25.00
2 in. conchas

No. 704......$26.50
2½ in. conchas

No. 706......$31.50
2 in. conchas

Nos. 706 and 708 have oval side pieces and bars very finely engraved.

No. 708......$47.50
2½ in. conchas

With solid gold bucking bronco and fancy silver buttons, extra fine close-link chains—the finest bit of this type made anywhere.

FINE SILVER MOUNTED HAND-FORGED BITS

No. 52.
$29.00

No. 48
$33.00

No. 47
$20.75

No. 46
$22.75

No. 44
$21.75

No. 43
$22.75

All Bits made either loose check or solid riveted, as desired. State which is preferred. The test of the thickness of the silver is the depth of the engraving—thin silver can not be engraved deep—our silver is thick and the engraving is deep.

DO NOT CUT OUT THE ENGRAVINGS—SEND NUMBERS ONLY

STEEL AND SILVER INLAID BITS
Hand Forged all in One Piece

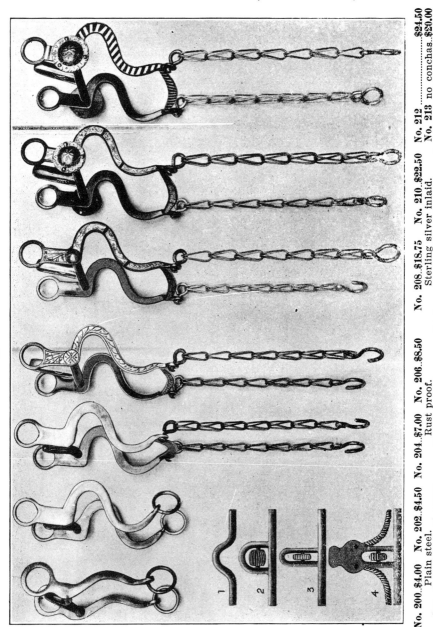

No. 200. $4.00   No. 202. $4.50   No. 204. $7.00   No. 206. $8.50   No. 208. $18.75   No. 210. $22.50   No. 212 ....$24.50

Plain steel.

Cuts showing style of mouth pieces used in our bits. No. 4, $1.00 extra in these bits.

Nos. 2 and 3 will cost 75c extra in Nos. 200, 202, 204 bits. Otherwise bits will be sent as shown in cuts.

Sterling silver inlaid.

Rust proof.

No. 213 no conchas. $20.00

We are showing an entirely new line of solid hand-forged steel, one-piece bits and spurs; no joints to work loose; made in our own shop. We know just how and of what material they are made—the best steel and pure, genuine silver, not the imitation or German silver used in most of the work sold out West. And it is deeply inlaid and put in to stay, not soft soldered on in the usual way. A superior piece of work in every way. All our bits and spurs fitted with rust-proof chains.

EXTRA FINE SILVER OVERLAID BITS

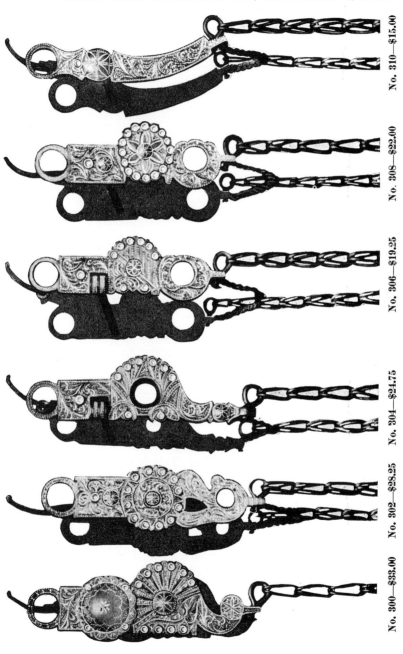

No. 300—$33.00   No. 302—$28.25   No. 304—$24.75   No. 306—$19.25   No. 308—$22.00   No. 310—$15.00

A line of work of extreme beauty, finish and durability. The face of the bit is completely covered with silver. There is no exposed metal to rust and spoil the appearance of a fine bit. Any of our silver inlaid bits can be made overlaid. Prices on application. Made either spade or half-breed mouthd mouth, and either loose or riveted jaws.

Silver overlaid bar at bottom with swivel chains, extra $5.00

HAND FORGED SILVER INLAID BITS

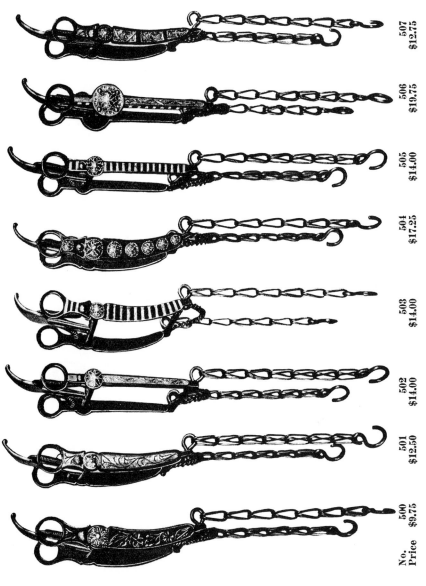

No. 500 / Price $9.75

501 / $12.50

502 / $14.00

503 / $14.00

504 / $17.25

505 / $14.00

506 / $19.75

507 / $12.75

A line of New Design Bits in Response to the demand for light-weight, serviceable bits moderately priced. With bottom bars, add $3.50 to price. Made half-breed month if so ordered.

DO NOT CUT OUT THE ENGRAVINGS—SEND NUMBERS ONLY

SILVER INLAID — HAND FORGED RING BITS

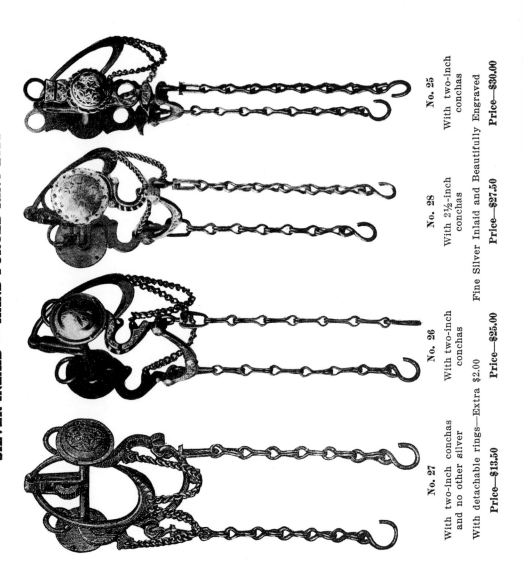

No. 25
With two-inch conchas
Fine Silver Inlaid and Beautifully Engraved
Price—$30.00

No. 28
With 2½-inch conchas
Price—$27.50

No. 26
With two-inch conchas
Price—$25.00

No. 27
With two-inch conchas
and no other silver
With detachable rings—Extra $2.00
Price—$13.50

BITS AND SPURS

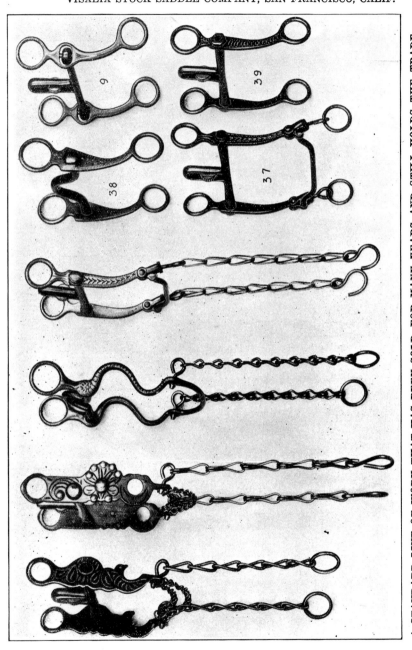

A STANDARD LINE OF WORK THAT HAS BEEN SOLD FOR MANY YEARS AND STILL HOLDS THE TRADE. GOOD STUFF WILL DO IT EVERY TIME

No. 710......$1.50
With bottom bar 1.75
No. 712.........$2.00
Spade Mouth.
With bottom bar 2.25

No. 714.........$2.75
No. 715.........$3.50
Spade mouth.

No. 719.........$1.35
Blued. All one piece.
Any of these bits
rust treated — 75c

No. 370.........$3.85
Rust treated. A
very superior bit
with hand - made
chains.

No.38, Above ..$1.60 No. 9, Above..$2.25
No.37, Below $2.60 No. 39, Below..$1.85

Any of the above will be rust treated
for 75c extra. Prices are for blue finish

EXTRA FINE SILVER INLAID HAND-FORGED SPURS

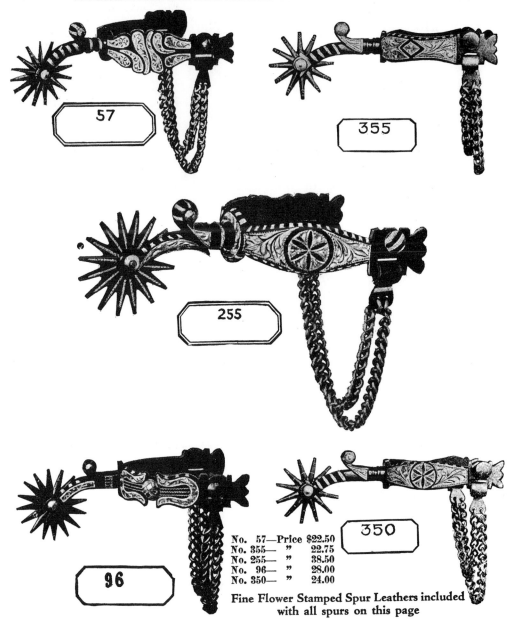

No. 57—Price $22.50
No. 355— " 22.75
No. 255— " 38.50
No. 96— " 28.00
No. 350— " 24.00

Fine Flower Stamped Spur Leathers included with all spurs on this page

OUR NEW "HEART" PATTERNS

MADE WITH EITHER STYLE SHANK AND ANY CURVE

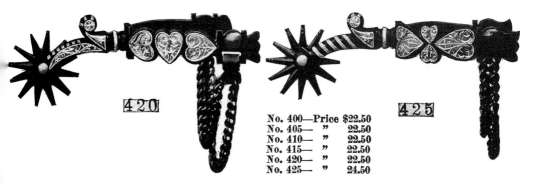

No. 400—Price $22.50
No. 405—   "   22.50
No. 410—   "   22.50
No. 415—   "   22.50
No. 420—   "   22.50
No. 425—   "   24.50

Any of our spurs made with raised or swing buttons if so ordered. Same price. Any spur made solid forged in one piece—$1.50 to $2.50 extra

FINE HAND-FORGED SILVER-MOUNTED SPURS

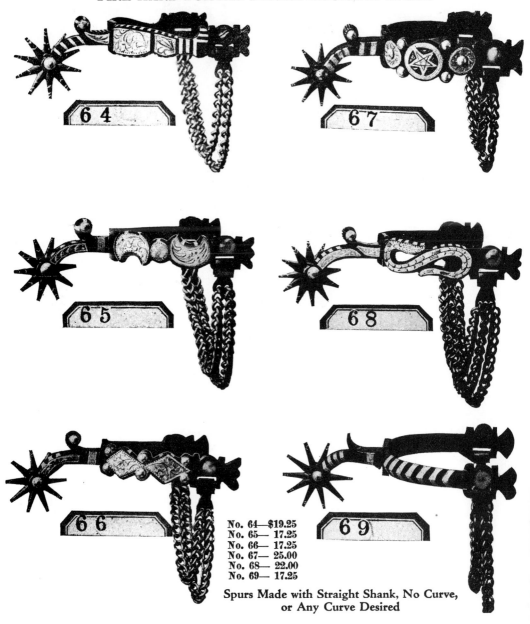

No. 64—$19.25
No. 65— 17.25
No. 66— 17.25
No. 67— 25.00
No. 68— 22.00
No. 69— 17.25

**Spurs Made with Straight Shank, No Curve,
or Any Curve Desired**

FINE HAND-FORGED SILVER-MOUNTED SPURS

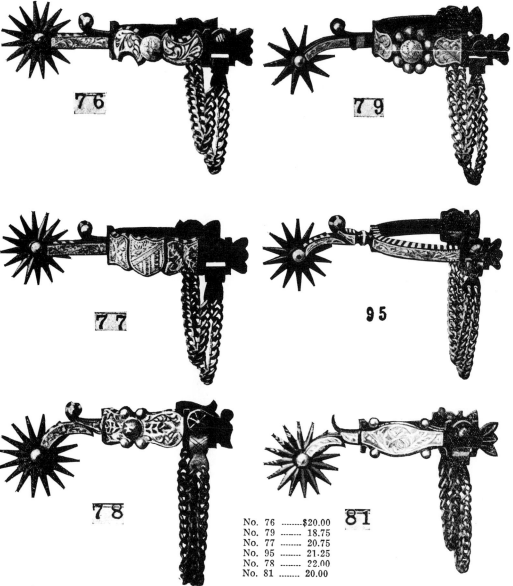

No. 76 ....$20.00	
No. 79 .... 18.75	
No. 77 .... 20.75	
No. 95 .... 21.25	
No. 78 .... 22.00	
No. 81 .... 20.00	

No malleable iron shanks or rowels used in our spurs. Everything is hand-forged in our own shop

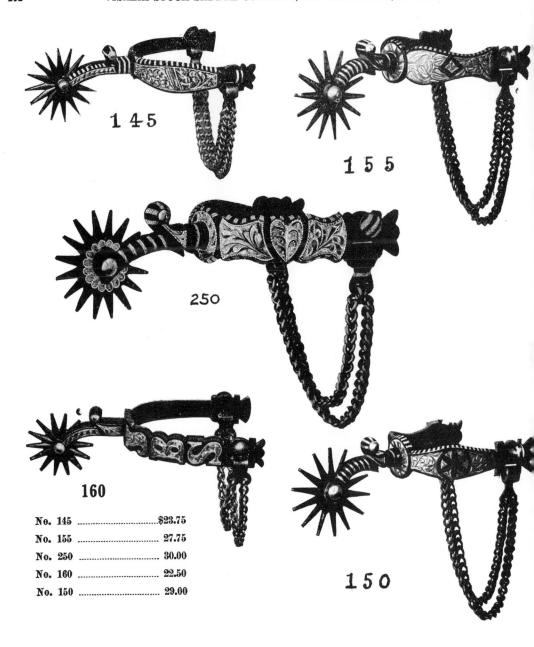

145

155

250

160

150

No. 145	$23.75
No. 155	27.75
No. 250	30.00
No. 160	22.50
No. 150	29.00

REPAIRING

Before

Broken
Battered — Useless

SPUR ROWELS

All our Rowels are hand forged and filed, not malleable iron, nor punched from sheet metal, as is usually the case, which leaves the prongs cross-grained and brittle.

SIZE	10	12	14	16
1½ to 2	$1.50	$2.00	$2.50	$3.00
2¼	2.00	2.50	3.00	3.50
2½	2.50	3.00	3.50	4.00
3	3.50	4.00	4.50	5.00

NEW MOUTHPIECES IN OLD BITS

We do an immense amount of this class of work and find that in most cases the breakage is not from accident or hard use but from rusting out. To eliminate this source of trouble, we have secured a new rustless steel that absolutely will not rust or corrode from any cause whatever, and will make a bit almost indestructable, except from accident.

The cost of these new mouthpieces is higher than the ordinary steel, as per the following list:

	Regular Steel	Rustless Steel
Half breed mouthpcs, riveted	$5.00	$6.00
Half breed mouthpcs, loose	6.00	7.00
Spade mouthpieces riveted	5.50	6.75
Spade mouthpieces, loose	6.50	7.75

These prices may vary somewhat if extra work is necessary.

Any of our new bits will be fitted with these rustless mouthpieces as follows:

Half breed mouthpieces (extra) $1.00
Spade mouthpieces (extra) 1.25

After
Repaired as good as new

STRAIGHT

⅛ CURVE

¼ CURVE

½ CURVE

FULL CURVE

Cut showing the various curve shanks we put on our spurs. Any spur in the catalog changed to suit you. If not specified, we send spurs just as shown in catalog. Knobs charged extra on spurs shown with hook: Plain, 75c; inlaid, $1.50.

We have unusual facilities for repairing and reclaiming old and apparently useless riding goods that would seem to have outlived their usefulness.

Almost every ranch has an old saddle, the leathers of which are good, but the tree is broken or hurts the horse—about as useless an article on a ranch as you can find. We will make a new tree to fit your old leathers, and put the old saddle back to work for you. It will pay you well. The cost of this work is not heavy. Write us about it.

Send in your old stuff and let us surprise you — If we can't repair it, it can't be repaired

ONE-PIECE HAND-FORGED SPURS
All Above Spurs Sterling Silver Mounted

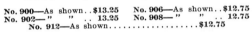

No. 900—As shown . . $13.25   No. 906—As shown . . $12.75
No. 902— ”   ” . . 13.25   No. 908— ”   ” . . 12.75
     No. 912—As shown $12.75

Spur Leathers — Hand Stamped

No. 4—Button . . . . $ .85   No. 5—Buckle $1.75
No. 3— ” . . . . 1.50   No. 4— ” 85
No. 1— ” . . . . 2.00   No. 3— ” 1.50
No. 6—Buckle 95   No. 1— ” 2.00

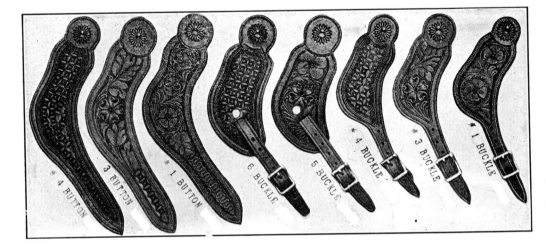

FINE HAND-BRAIDED HAIR HAT BANDS

Width	Plain No Silver	Silver Sterling Silver Mounts
⅝-inch	$1.15	$1.50
1-inch	1.50	2.00

Fine Braided Horse Hair Natural Colors

BUCKING ROLL

Medium, 3 inches high	$3.50
High, 4 inches high	3.75
Extra high, 5 inches high	4.00

strings or billets to screw on
Made with holes for the

LEATHER HAT BANDS

No. 1—⅝-in. embossed .35
No. 2—½-in. " .25
No. 3—⅜-in. " .25
No. 4—¼-in. flat or round .25
No. 5—Braided 1.75
Black, Pearl, Tan, Brown

HAIR HATBANDS

LEATHER HAT BANDS

RUST TREATED BIT CHAINS

Steel — Hand Made

	No Swivel	With Swivel
7-link	$1.15	$1.60
10-link	1.35	1.85

German Silver
(Swivels and all)

These are all our own make of best materials. No cast iron swivels used. The German silver chains are extra fine, all silver soldered. A fine finish to a fine bit.

Any of the above silver-plated with swivel......$1.00 extra
no swivel........ .75 extra

Monel Metal same price as German Silver. This metal is rustproof, strong as steel, not affected by acids, and does not tarnish.

Curb Chain   Bit Chain   Spur Chain

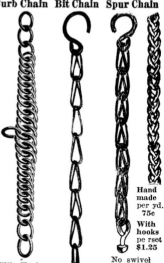

Hand made per yd. 75c
With hooks pe rset $1.25

No swivel

With swivel

DEPENDABLE SPURS

No. 700	$2.50
No. 702	2.75
No. 703	2.50
No. 706	2.75

With Hooks
Solid Link
Medium, 75c
Solid Nickle
$1.75

HAND-FORGED SPURS—PLAIN AND SILVER INLAID

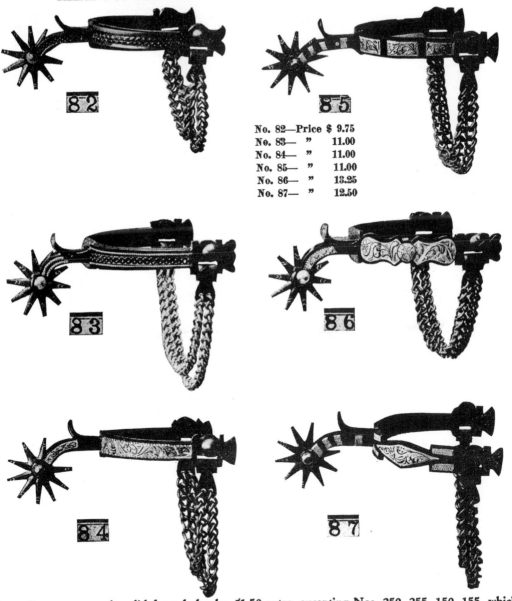

No. 82—Price $ 9.75
No. 83— ”   11.00
No. 84— ”   11.00
No. 85— ”   11.00
No. 86— ”   13.25
No. 87— ”   12.50

Any of our spurs made solid forged shanks, $1.50 extra, excepting Nos. 250, 255, 150, 155, which are $2.50 extra

FINE STERLING SILVER MOUNTED HEADSTALLS

NOTICE A line of fine bridles that are not equaled by any—We make a specialty of fine silver work saddles, bridles, martingales, bits, spurs, etc., and have unexcelled facilities for turning out specialties in this line, something different from the ordinary. Write us about it.

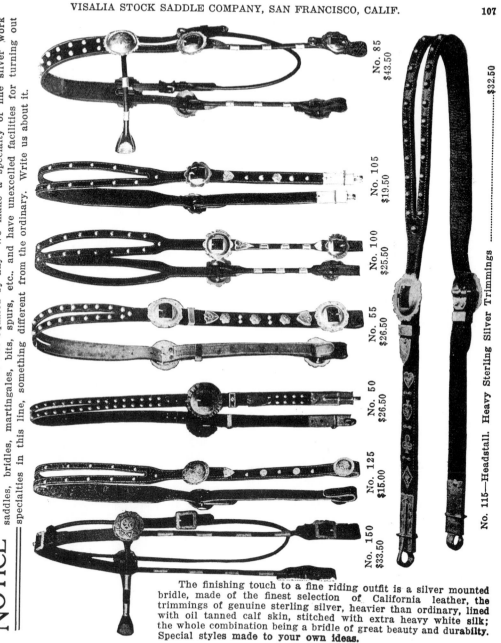

No. 85 $43.50

No. 105 $19.50

No. 100 $25.50

No. 55 $26.50

No. 50 $26.50

No. 125 $15.00

No. 150 $33.50

No. 115—Headstall. Heavy Sterling Silver Trimmings $32.50

The finishing touch to a fine riding outfit is a silver mounted bridle, made of the finest selection of California leather, the trimmings of genuine sterling silver, heavier than ordinary, lined with oil tanned calf skin, stitched with extra heavy white silk; the whole combination being a bridle of great beauty and durabilty. Special styles made to your own ideas.

STERLING SILVER MOUNTED HEADSTALLS (All except No. 244 are hand-sewed rounds)

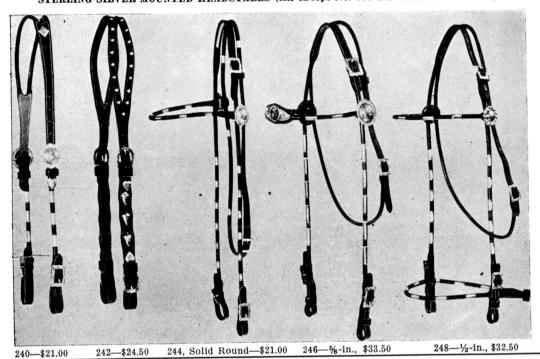

240—$21.00   242—$24.50   244, Solid Round—$21.00   246—⅝-in., $33.50   248—½-in., $32.50

HUMANE HEADSTALLS—Don't pinch the ears. Nickle trimmed

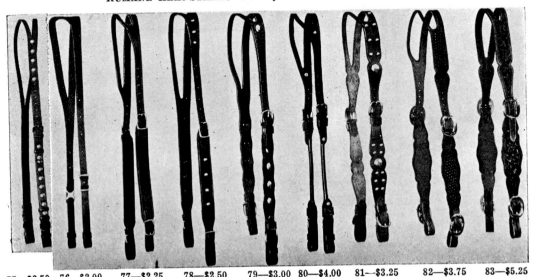

75—$2.50   76—$2.00   77—$2.25   78—$2.50   79—$3.00   80—$4.00   81—$3.25   82—$3.75   83—$5.25

HEAD STALLS

Round   **Black**

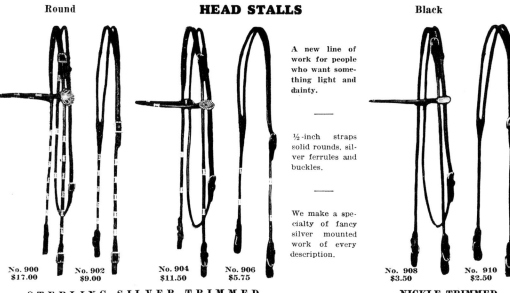

A new line of work for people who want something light and dainty.

———

½-inch straps solid rounds, silver ferrules and buckles.

———

We make a specialty of fancy silver mounted work of every description.

No. 900 $17.00
No. 902 $9.00
No. 904 $11.50
No. 906 $5.75
No. 908 $3.50
No. 910 $2.50

STERLING SILVER TRIMMED   **NICKLE TRIMMED**
HEADSTALLS—All except 15 and 195 lined and silk stitched

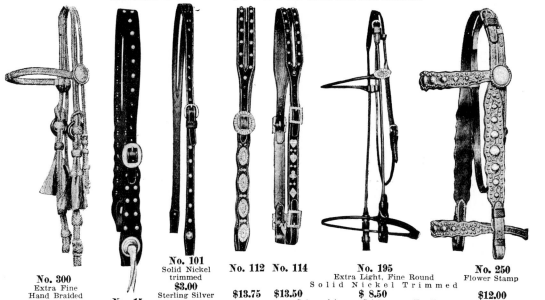

No. 300
Extra Fine
Hand Braided
Rawhide
$8.50

No. 15
$2.75

No. 101
Solid Nickel
trimmed
$3.00
Sterling Silver
trimmed
$8.75

No. 112   No. 114
$13.75 $13.50
$22.00 $20.00

No. 195
Extra Light, Fine Round
Solid Nickel Trimmed
$8.50
Sterling Silver Trimmed
$16.75

No. 250
Flower Stamp
$12.00
$36.75

HAND-SEWED HEADSTALLS—SELECTED LEATHER

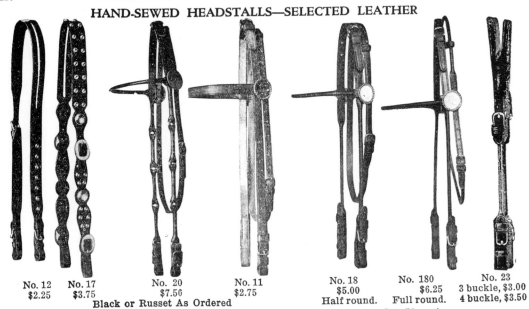

No. 12	No. 17	No. 20	No. 11	No. 18	No. 180	No. 23
$2.25	$3.75	$7.50	$2.75	$5.00	$6.25	3 buckle, $3.00
				Half round.	Full round.	4 buckle, $3.50

Black or Russet As Ordered
Any of the above with bosals charged extra.   Round, $1.00; flat, 50 cents

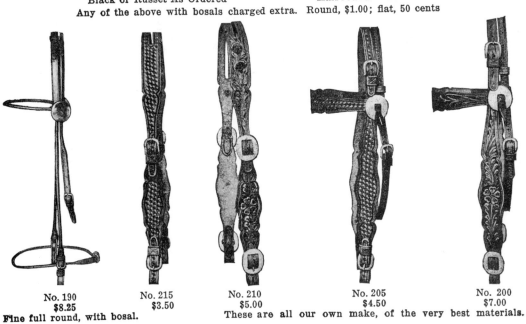

No. 190	No. 215	No. 210	No. 205	No. 200
$8.25	$3.50	$5.00	$4.50	$7.00

Fine full round, with bosal.   These are all our own make, of the very best materials.

COLLAR MARTINGALES   **QUIRTS**

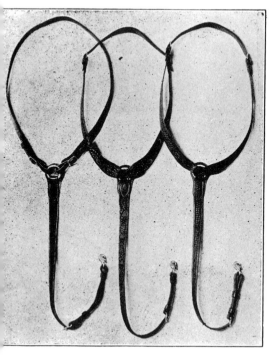

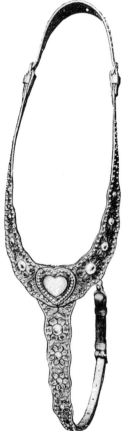

No. 110   No. 118   No. 120

No. 50   No. 52   No. 54

$2.25 $2.75 $3.50

RAWHIDE HACKAMORES

No. 110 . . . . . . **$4.50**
Plain.

No. 111 . . . . . . **$5.00**
Nickle spots.

No. 118 . . . . . . **$6.50**
Flower stamp.

No. 120 . . . . . . **$4.50**
Basket stamp.

No. 125 . . . . . . **$4.00**
Plain.

No. 127 . . . . . **$4.50**
Plain with nickle
spots.

These Collar Mar-
tingales are self-ad-
justing, with a leath-
er safe under the
ring.

No. 110 has the
adjustment at the
ring as shown.

ngle
se,
lid
ot
ather
ad.

	Single	Double
12 strand. .	$3.50	135 . . $4.50
8 strand. .	2.75	140 . . 3.50
6 strand. .	2.25	145 . . 3.15
4 strand. .	2.00	150 . . 2.75
		Tail Mane

r Feadores, ext., put on, $2.00-$2.50

No. 112. Full flower
stamp, Sterling silver.
all lined and silk stitched
. . . .**$37.50**
No. 114. Like No. 112, sol-
id nickle trimmed, lined
and stitched **$13.75**
No. 115. Not lined....**$11.50**
No. 116. Same as above but
bskt stamped not lin'd $7.50
No. 117. Same as above,
but basket stamped; not
lined, no nickle buttons....
. . . .**$5.50**

Shot loaded. Made **heavy,**
medium and light. **Sent**
medium weight if not **spe-**
cified. Average length **body**
part, 16 inches.

Short size, 15 inches; **long**
size, 17 inches. Made **any**
other length to order.

All our rawhide work **is**
hand made and of **selected**
material. No split hide **used**

Any Special Style Made To Order

HAND MADE RAWHIDE REINS
Our own make, and guaranteed all grain stock—No splits used.

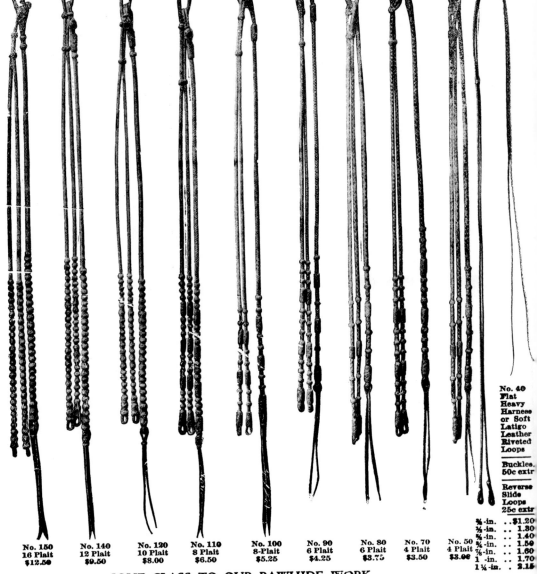

No. 150 16 Plait $12.50	No. 140 12 Plait $9.50	No. 120 10 Plait $8.00	No. 110 8 Plait $6.50	No. 100 8-Plait $5.25	No. 90 6 Plait $4.25	No. 80 6 Plait $3.75	No. 70 4 Plait $3.50	No. 50 4 Plait $3.00

No. 40
Flat
Heavy
Harness
or Soft
Latigo
Leather
Riveted
Loops

Buckles,
50c extr

Reverse
Slide
Loops
25c extr

⅜-in.	. .	$1.20
½-in.	. .	1.30
⅝-in.	. .	1.40
¾-in.	. .	1.50
⅞-in.	. .	1.60
1 -in.	. .	1.70
1¼-in.	. .	2.15

SOME CLASS TO OUR RAWHIDE WORK

FORK AND CANTLE RIMS
Heavy Sterling Silver
Plain Edge,
No engraving.
Fork $20.00
Cantle 24.50
Scalloped Edge
Engraved
Fork $23.50
Cantle 27.50

STERLING SILVER NAME PLATES
Banner Pattern
3 Initials
Large $12.00
Medium 9.00
Small 7.00
More than three initials charged extra.

Extra-Fine 8-Power Binoculars, with leather case and strap. No. 250 - $17.50

STIRRUP BOLTS—1¼-in. STERLING SILVER CONCHA HEADS

NO. 60   NO. 65   NO. 70   NO. 75   SILVER CAP NO. 80

No. 150—MILITARY FIELD GLASSES—$8.50

STERLING SILVER CONCHA BOLTS
Solid Bronze Stirrup Bolts with Sterling Silver Heads Securely Attached
Complete with brass nuts and washers—Prices per pair

No. 60—1¼-in..$3.25   No. 70—1¼-in..$3.50   No. 80— ⅞-in..$1.25
No. 65—1¼-in..$3.75   No. 75—1¼-in..$3.25   Other Sizes in Proportion

HEAVY STERLING SILVER SKIRT CORNERS

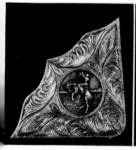

No. 500—BRONCO

No.	Price each Not Engraved
No. 1—1¾-inch	$1.75
No. 2—2¼-inch	2.25
No. 3—2¾-inch	3.00
No. 4—3¼-inch	3.75
No. 5—3¾-inch	5.00
No. 6—TAP	6.50

Nos. 500 and 502 Same Prices

No. 502 STEER or HORSE HEAD

No.	As Shown	Gold Head
1	$2.75	$ 5.75
2	3.75	8.25
3	4.75	9.50
4	6.00	10.50
5	7.25	11.50
6—TAP	8.75	13.50

No. 504—RAISED CENTER

No.	Price each As shown	Gold horse
1—3½-in.	.$ 3.75	$ 8.00
2—4⅛-in.	7.00	11.25
3—5¼-in.	10.75	15.00
4—TAP	12.00	16.25

No. 506—LONGHORN

No.	Price each As shown	Gold head
1—2½-in.	.$4.50	$11.25
2—2¾-in.	5.25	12.00
3—3¼-in.	6.00	12.75
4—3½-in.	6.75	13.50
5—TAP	9.00	15.75

A small charge will be made for installing silver corners on saddle.

Extra Heavy Sterling Silver   **– CONCHAS –**   **Loops Silver Soldered On**

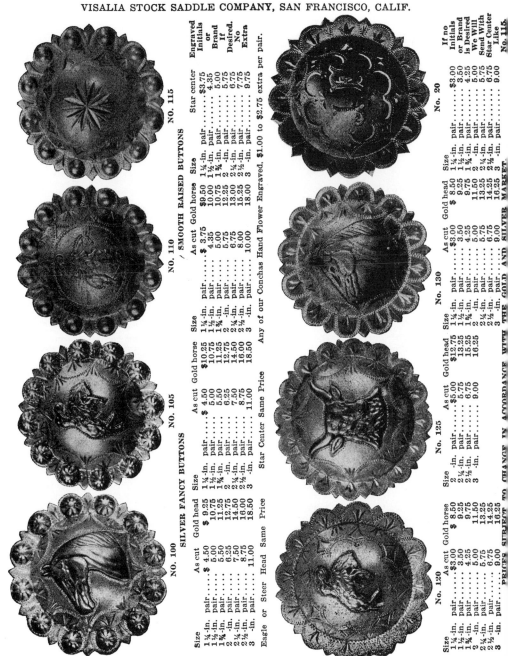

SILVER FANCY BUTTONS

NO. 100

Size		As cut	Gold head
1¼-in.	pair..	$ 4.50	$ 9.25
1½-in.	pair..	5.00	10.75
1¾-in.	pair..	5.50	11.25
2 -in.	pair..	6.25	12.75
2¼-in.	pair..	7.50	14.50
2½-in.	pair..	8.75	16.00
3 -in.	pair..	11.00	18.50

Eagle or Steer Head Same Price

NO. 105

Size		As cut	Gold horse
1¼-in.	pair..	$ 4.50	$10.25
1½-in.	pair..	5.00	10.75
1¾-in.	pair..	5.50	11.25
2 -in.	pair..	6.25	12.75
2¼-in.	pair..	7.50	14.50
2½-in.	pair..	8.75	16.00
3 -in.	pair..	11.00	18.50

Star Center Same Price

SMOOTH RAISED BUTTONS

NO. 110

Size		As cut	Gold horse
1¼-in.	pair..	$ 3.75	$9.50
1½-in.	pair..	4.35	10.00
1¾-in.	pair..	5.00	10.75
2 -in.	pair..	5.75	12.25
2¼-in.	pair..	6.75	13.00
2½-in.	pair..	8.00	15.25
3 -in.	pair..	10.00	18.00

NO. 115

Size		Star center
1¼-in.	pair..	$3.75
1½-in.	pair..	4.35
1¾-in.	pair..	5.00
2 -in.	pair..	5.75
2¼-in.	pair..	6.75
2½-in.	pair..	7.75
3 -in.	pair..	9.75

Engraved Initials or Brand If Desired. No Extra

Any of our Conchas Hand Flower Engraved, $1.00 to $2.75 extra per pair.

No. 120

Size		As cut	Gold horse
1¼-in.	pair..	$3.00	$ 8.50
1½-in.	pair..	3.50	9.25
1¾-in.	pair..	4.25	9.75
2 -in.	pair..	5.00	11.50
2¼-in.	pair..	5.75	13.25
2½-in.	pair..	6.75	14.25
3 -in.	pair..	9.00	16.25

No. 125

Size		As cut	Gold head
2 -in.	pair..	$5.00	$12.75
2¼-in.	pair..	5.75	13.25
2½-in.	pair..	6.75	15.25
3 -in.	pair..	9.00	16.25

No. 130

Size		As cut	Gold head
1¼-in.	pair..	$3.00	$ 8.50
1½-in.	pair..	3.50	9.25
1¾-in.	pair..	4.25	9.75
2 -in.	pair..	5.00	11.50
2¼-in.	pair..	5.75	13.25
2½-in.	pair..	6.75	14.25
3 -in.	pair..	9.00	16.25

No. 20

If no Initials or Brand Is Desired We Will Send With Star Center Like No. 115

PRICES SUBJECT TO CHANGE IN ACCORDANCE WITH THE GOLD AND SILVER MARKET

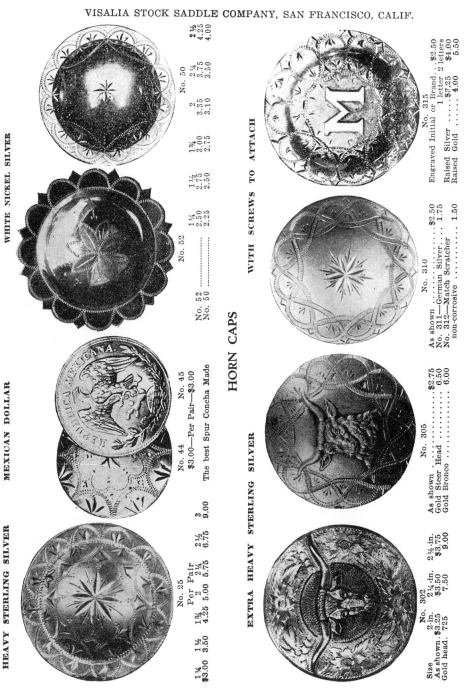

CONCHAS

HEAVY STERLING SILVER   MEXICAN DOLLAR   WHITE NICKEL SILVER

No. 25
Per Pair
1⅛ 1½ 2 2¼ 2½
$3.00 3.50 4.25 5.00 5.75 6.75 9.00

No. 44   No. 45
$3.00—Per Pair—$3.00
The best Spur Concha Made

No. 52
No. 52 .... 1⅜ 1½ 1¾ 2 2¼ 2½
No. 50 .... 2.50 2.75 3.00 3.35 3.75 4.25
       .... 2.25 2.50 2.75 3.10 3.50 4.00

No. 50

EXTRA HEAVY STERLING SILVER   WITH SCREWS TO ATTACH

HORN CAPS

No. 302
Size   2-in. 2¾-in. 2½-in.
As shown. $3.25 $3.50 $3.75
Gold head. 7.25   7.50   9.00

No. 305
As shown $2.75
Gold Steer Head 6.50
Gold Bronco 6.00

No. 310
As shown $2.50
No. 311—German Silver 1.75
No. 312—Match Scratcher
non-corrosive 1.50

No. 315
Engraved Initial or Brand.. $2.50
    1 letter 2 letters
Raised Silver $3.25 $4.00
Raised Gold 4.00   5.50

SILVER MOUNTED EQUIPMENT

We have complete facilities for fitting up silver-mounted saddles, bridles, martingales and other riding gear, and will be pleased to furnish all information to anyone in need of such equipment.

No. 205—Heavy
1¼-inch per pair........$2.50
1½-inch per pair........ 3.00
1¾-inch per pair........ 3.50
2 -inch per pair........ 4.00

No. 215—Heavy
1¼-inch per pair........$1.80
1½-inch per pair........ 2.25
1¾-inch per pair........ 2.85
2 -inch per pair........ 3.50

No. 200—Extra Heavy
1¼-inch per pair........$4.25
1½-inch per pair........ 4.75
1¾-inch per pair........ 5.25
2 -inch per pair........ 6.00

No. 210—heavy
1¼-inch per pair........$1.80
1½-inch per pair........ 2.25
1¾-inch per pair........ 2.85
2 -inch per pair........ 3.50

All Our Conchos are Made of Extra Heavy Sterling Silver Engraved by Hand

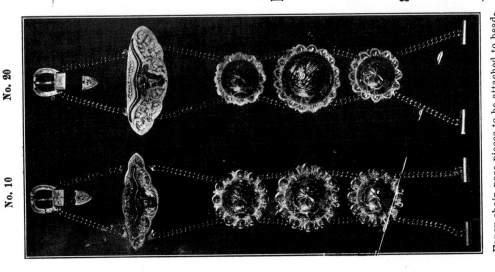

No. 20

No. 10

Fancy chain nose pieces to be attached to headstall from brow band to nose band. Conchos and buckles made of heavy sterling silver.

No. 10—Raised buttons on conchos...$26.00

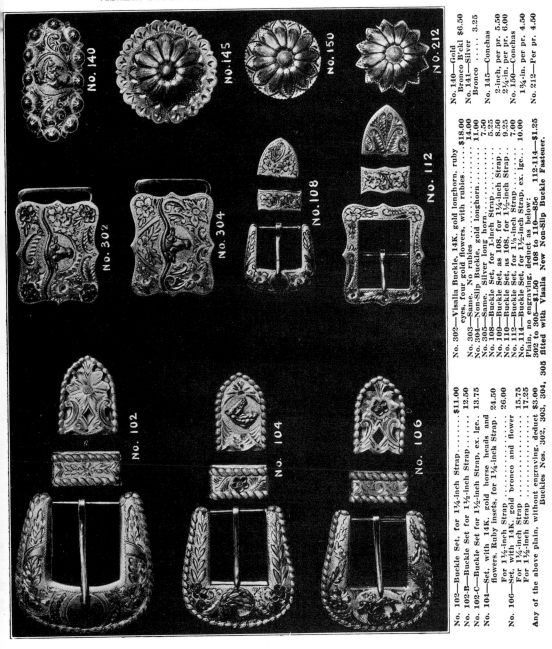

No. 102—Buckle Set, for 1¼-inch Strap......$11.00
No. 102-B—Buckle Set for 1½-inch Strap...... 12.50
No. 102-C—Buckle Set for 1½-inch Strap, ex. lge. 13.75
No. 104—Set, with 14K. gold horse heads and
    flowers. Ruby insets, for 1¼-inch Strap. 24.50
    For 1½-inch Strap 26.00
No. 106—Set, with 14K. gold bronco and flower
    For 1¼-inch Strap 15.75
    For 1½-inch Strap 17.25
Any of the above plain, without engraving, deduct $3.00

No. 302—Visalia Buckle, 14K. gold longhorn, ruby
    eyes, four gold flowers, with rubies.....$18.00
No. 303—Same. No rubies 14.00
No. 304—Non-Slip Buckle, gold longhorn...... 11.00
No. 305—Same. Silver long horn............. 7.50
No. 108—Buckle Set, for 1-inch Strap........ 5.25
No. 109—Buckle Set, as 108, for 1¼-inch Strap. 8.50
No. 110—Buckle Set, as 108, for 1¼-inch Strap. 9.25
No. 112—Buckle Set, for 1½-inch Strap....... 7.00
No. 114—Buckle Set, for 1½-inch Strap, ex. lge. 10.00
Plain, no engraving, deduct as below:
302 to 305—$1.50   108 to 110—85c   112-114—$1.25
Buckles Nos. 302, 303, 304, 305 fitted with Visalia New Non-Slip Buckle Fastener.

No. 140—Gold
    Bronco B'ckl $6.50
No. 141—Silver
    Bronco 3.25
No. 145—Conchas
    2-inch, per pr. 5.50
    2¼-in. per pr. 6.00
No. 150—Conchas
    1¾-in. per pr. 4.50
No. 212—Per pr. 4.50

COMMENTS OF A VETERINARIAN

Anthrax occurs in most parts of the world and is one of the most dangerous diseases. The germ which causes this infection forms spores which may live in the soil as long as twenty-five years. If these spores are inhaled, eaten with food, or come in contact with an open wound, they may enter the blood. Once they find their way to the blood stream, they multiply very rapidly, and in the most susceptible animals, produce death within twenty-four hours.

In man, anthrax is not highly fatal, being most dangerous if infection occurs around the face or neck. This may occur by wounds to the face or neck becoming infected; or due to bites from mosquitoes or flies which have been feeding on an infected animal or contaminated discharges. The most common form in man is a severe carbuncle (boil) at the point of infection. Inflammation may extend over a considerable area and after about thirty-six hours the center of the pustule may become brown. Usually there is no fever. The swelling may be slight or extensive. The cases with marked swelling, especially of the face, are more likely to be fatal. Inhalation infections occur more commonly among those sorting and cleaning hair and wool, and is known as "Wool-Sorter's Disease." The attack is sudden with chills and fever. Breathing is rapid and often painful. Death usually occurs between the third and fifth days.

The following history illustrates the danger connected with handling dead animals. A Veterinarian had completed a post-mortem examination of a dead cow. Rubber gloves were worn and great care was taken not to get blood or discharges on himself. He had completed the examination and while washing was bitten on the hand by a mosquito. A carbuncle developed but he was fortunate enough to have serum administered promptly and it was not fatal.

Another interesting case occurred in a bull recently shipped a considerable distance. As usual, he fought, scratching and bruising himself in several places. Upon arrival at the destination he was placed in a pen and being restless he pawed a great deal, throwing the dirt over his back. A few days later he died of anthrax. No doubt the spores were dug up with the dirt and entered the body through some of the scratch wounds on his back. It was known that many cattle on this farm had died from anthrax. (The heaviest losses occurred fifteen years previous.) The carcasses were buried in shallow pits but the anthrax spores lived on and caused the death of this fine animal. This serves to emphasize the importance of carefully burning all carcasses where anthrax is suspected.

Fortunately very satisfactory vaccines are available, although the reliable products are reasonably expensive. The spore vaccines are dangerous. They should be used only by properly trained veterinarians, and only then with the greatest of care.

1. A serum protects the individual for a short time only.
2. A true vaccine or virus produces the disease, although the attack may be very mild.
3. A combination of serum and virus properly administered gives good protection in some diseases.
4. Bacterins and aggressins do not cause the disease, but stimulate the protective forces of the body against a certain infection. Some of these products are very effective in preventing certain diseases, but for others they have little or no value.
5. Vaccination may be harmful if the individual is sick or in a weakened condition. In severe outbreaks, an especially powerful vaccine may be necessary to control the infection. Losses may continue for about two weeks following vaccination since about this much time is required for the animal body to respond to vaccination.
6. It is good policy to avoid transportation, fatigue, exposure, overfeeding, or sudden change in food for at least a week following vaccination. It is also good management to have the animals in thrifty condition before vaccination.
7. Some vaccines are dangerous in that they may cause the disease in man or animals. The bottles should be burned or carefully sterilized. Should any be spilled, disinfect the area immediately.
8. The services of a qualified veterinarian is good insurance.

COWBOY BELTS

No. 250—As shown, 7½ inches wide....$8.75   No. 251—All basket stamp....$5.00   No. 252—Plain....$4.50

BELTS DE LUXE

No. 600—BELT

1¾-inches wide,
1¼-in. Sterling
Silver buckle
set

$18.50

No. 601—BELT

1½-inches wide,
1-inch Sterling
Silver buckle
$17.50

Fine Grade Light Walker Saddle Leather—Extra fine flower stamp. Black back ground, showing the pattern up in strong relief. Calf lined and silk stitched. A strikingly beautiful belt. Sterling silver rope edge buckle set. A classy piece of work throughout.

No. 602 BELT—Beautiful Oak leaf and acorn stamp with black background. Lined and stitched.

1¾-in. Sterling Silver buckle set
with gold horse head—$23.00
with silver horse head—$20.75

No. 604 BELT—Fine rose stamp belt with black background, lined and stitched.—1½-in. Sterling Silver buckle set — $12.75
(This belt shows the No. 108 sterling silver buckle set, page 117.)

SADDLE LEATHER BELTS—FINE STOCK—HAND SEWED

No. 500—1⅛ inch. Fine hand stamp. Rose pattern. Extra heavy sterling silver buckle, floral design....$7.00

No. 504—1¼ inch. Fine hand flower stamp, nickle plated buckle $4.00

No. 506—1½ inch. Attractive floral patterns; nickle plated buckle $1.75

No. 508—1¼ inch. Flower pattern nickle buckle $1.50

No. 502—1 inch. Fine rosebud hand flower stamp. Sterling silver buckle with gold horse and rider.....$9.00

No. 510—1 inch. Neat flower design; solid nickle buckle.
....$1.75

No. 514—1¼-inch. Basket stamp nickle buckle.....$1.50

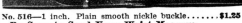

No. 512—1¼ inch. Snake pattern, nickle buckle....$1.50

No. 516—1 inch. Plain smooth nickle buckle.......$1.25

All Belts Russet Leather—Black, If Ordered—Be Sure to Send Your Waist Measure

Levi Strauss

WAIST OVERALLS
'RIDERS' JACKETS

"TOPS" on Every
Range for 70 Years

LEVI'S were styled in the days when every one rode . . . were actually tailor-made 'to fit the saddle . . . and that's why they're still the favorite of the hard-riding cowboy. In fact, LEVI'S blue jeans and Rider's Jackets have for years made up the complete work outfits of thousands of real Westerners. Built for HARD WEAR . . . they are made of the finest . . . toughest . . . heaviest denim—loomed expressly for LEVI'S. Stitched with EXTRA-TEST special thread—so strong you get this unconditional GUARANTEE—A NEW PAIR IF THEY RIP!

Lot 506xx—$1.95 each

LEVI'S RIDER'S JACKET TO
Match Lot 501xx

Look at the picture — Roomy at the shoulder . . . stitched pleated front so you can let it out if you like more room. Snug at the waist for riding comfort — back-strap permits further adjustment . . . one big front pocket. Can be worn open or closed-collar type.

NEW PATENTED
LEVI'S with non-scratch **CONCEALED RIVET** on back pockets

X-RAY Diagram of Levi's patented concealed rivet

GUARANTEED
A new pair
FREE
if they rip!

THE RIVETS ARE STILL THERE —BUT YOU CAN'T SEE THEM

Lot 501xx—$1.75 ea.
LEVI'S Famous No. 501xx Heavy Blue Denim Waist Overalls. Five pockets.

Lot 201 Men's — $1.50 ea.
Lot 203 Youth's — $1.40 ea.
Up to 30 in. Made like 501xx in 9-oz. Denim.

TWO HORSE BRAND TRADE MARK
LEVI STRAUSS & CO.

LEVI'S are cut like tailor-made pants, and in 70 years this "cut" has never been successfully copied. Their leadership is so secure that more Overalls are cut to "look like" LEVI'S than all others combined!

also . . .
LEVI'S for Ladies!

FOR WORK AND PLAY OUTDOORS

A REAL OVERALL . . . made of a new full-weight, soft-weave Denim . . . smart and trim. Carefully tailored to give proper style, hip-fit and comfort to the feminine wearer. Fills that need for a tough outdoor garment that will take punishment . . . yet leave you looking "dressed" and feeling fit.

Lot 401—$1.75 each

Levi Strauss De Luxe
PRICE $7.50   Sizes 14½ to 17½ 34½ inch Sleeve Only

WORSTED TWILL SHIRTS

This is a Lorraine Fabric . . . 100 per cent Virgin Wool . . . woven into a fine soft twill . . . as light and warm as silk. Made with a 3½-inch collar . . . it has smart, snappy angled pockets and pocket flaps . . . full sleeves neatly gathered into a snug-fitting, stylish, 3-button cuff . . . at an agle to match pockets. A wide selection of colors (ball buttons to match).

No. 6992—Royal Blue	No. 6997—Terra Cotta
No. 6994—Pearl Grey	No. 6998—Navy Blue
No. 6995—Fawn	No. 6999—Light Green

No. 6993—Jet Black (with white ball buttons) ☞

Levi Strauss BUCKAROO SHIRTS — JACKETS *and* CALIFORNIA PANTS — *Pendleton Fabrics*

Pommel Slicker

Made of extra heavy pure wool Pendleton Fabric . . . So tightly woven that it is practically wind and storm proof. A soft dark brown plaid to match California Pants (Shown on page 50)

☞ **No. 200-X Shirt—Price $7.50**

TARPS

SPECIAL LOW PRICES SUBJECT TO CHANGE WITHOUT NOTICE

Feet	10 oz.	12 oz.	15 oz.	18 oz.	21 oz.
6x15	$5.75	$7.00	$8.50	$9.75	10.75
6x16	6.00	7.25	9.00	10.25	11.50
6x17	6.50	7.75	9.50	11.00	12.00
7x15	—	—	10.25	11.50	12.75
7x16	—	—	10.75	12.25	13.50
7x17	—	—	11.25	13.00	14.25
7x18	—	—	11.75	13.50	15.25

Every one is made of one solid piece of duck, no seams. This will appeal to those who have had a wet experience with leaky center seams. Made with snaps and rings.

Copyright, 1910, by A. J. Tower Co.

Plain white paulins, made of duck without seams. Furnished with snaps and rings or grommets.

TOWER'S FISH BRAND

No. 6700—Jacket....$13.50
Has new adjustable bottom (not knitted) . . . convertible two-way collar (open or closed) . . . two vertical slash pockets and button cuffs.

TOWER'S SLICKERS

Size 0	Chest 44-46 in. — Length 62 in.
Size 1	Chest 41-43 in. — Length 61 in.
Size 2	Chest 38-40 in. — Length 59 in.
Size 3	Chest 35-37 in. — Length 57 in.

Price $6.00

This cartoon, intended solely to call your attention to the Jo Mora Map
and Poster described on the opposite page, does not appear on the
Poster, and is no part of it.

JO MORA'S MAP AND POSTER

igan, you cowboys, outdoor hombres and students of the West!

Here's the best concentrated essence of Cowboy Lore ever hazed out of the old range. THE JO MORA COWBOY AND RODEO MAP! It's 25 by 31 inches, done in full colors, and it gives you the full ev-

olution of the Cowboy from the old Spanish Conquistador who first brought beef to America, right down to the Rodeo Rider of today. It pictures the changes in stock saddles from the first to the latest; also the spurs, bits, chaps, and all that makes up a Cowboy's working gear; how they rope and brand, and all the rodeo sports. Then to chase the blues away, you'll get a kick out of the bird's-eye view of the rodeo field in full swing, done in Jo Mora's inimitable humorous manner. The depression will not bother you after you have given it the once over. And you can hogtie and brand one of there for your own, postpaid and rolled in a tube, for ONE U. S. dollar (no matter what its value may be the day you send it), and it will doll up your bunk house, front parlor, or den like nobody's business. Here's a real cowboy pictorial dictionary and blues dispeller, colorful, decorative, and instructive. It's as interesting to the old-timers as it is to the kids. Send us your dollar and address, and we will do the rest. You'll like it!

$1.00, Postpaid, When Cash Accompanies Order

Visalia Stock Saddle Co. — 2123 Market Street — San Francisco, California

RUSSELL'S PICTURES

A MOST ATTRACTIVE SET OF INTERESTING PICTURES TO ADORN YOUR WALLS OR TABLE

"THE BOLTER"

DON'T
OVER-
LOOK
THIS
OFFER!

Set of 12 Famous

Charles Russell's

Cowboy Pictures

beautifully colored

for only

$2.50

CHARLES M. RUSSELL
The Greatest Cowboy Artist the World Has Produced

POSTAGE PREPAID WHEN
CASH ACCOMPANIES ORDER

"COWBOY LIFE"

"A Bronk to Breakfast"—Bucking bronco with rider plunging through cook's fire, knocking utensils right and left, spilling contents. Cook panning the rider.

IN WITHOUT KUOCKING	SINGLE HANDED
THE FIRST WAGON TRAIL	WHERE IGNORANCE IS BLISS
AMBUSHED	A DISPUTED TRAIL
A SEROUS PREDICAMENT	AT CLOSE QUARTERS

A DANGEROUS CRIPPLE

Sole Distributors

Visalia Stock Saddle Co. — 2123 Market Street — San Francisco, California

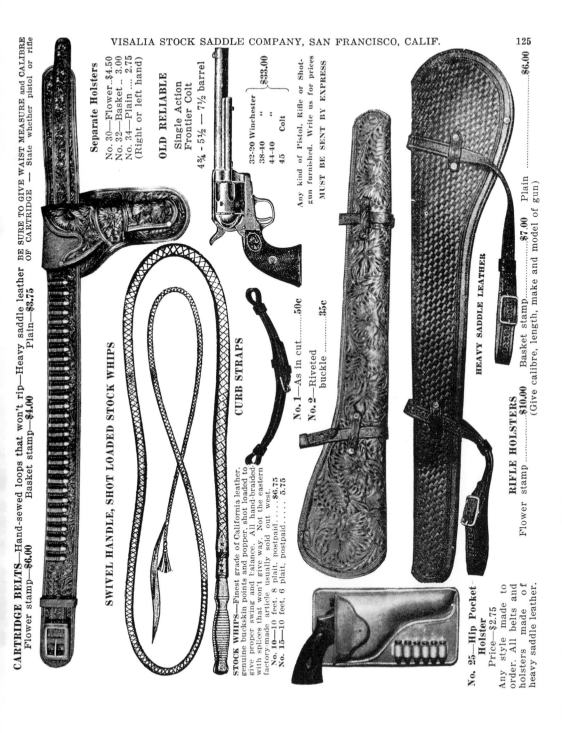

CARTRIDGE BELTS.—Hand-sewed loops that won't rip—Heavy saddle leather. BE SURE TO GIVE WAIST MEASURE and CALIBRE OF CARTRIDGE — State whether pistol or rifle

Plain—$3.75
Basket stamp—$4.00
Flower stamp—$6.00

SWIVEL HANDLE, SHOT LOADED STOCK WHIPS

STOCK WHIPS—Finest grade of California leather, genuine buckskin points and popper, shot loaded to give proper swing and balance. All hand-braided with splices that won't give way. Not the eastern factory-made article usually sold out west.

No. 10—10 feet, 8 plait, postpaid.... $6.75
No. 15—10 feet, 6 plait, postpaid.... 5.75

CURB STRAPS

No. 1—As in cut........50c
No. 2—Riveted buckle 35c

Separate Holsters

No. 30—Flower..$4.50
No. 32—Basket.. 3.00
No. 34—Plain.... 2.75
(Right or left hand)

OLD RELIABLE

Single Action
Frontier Colt
4¾ - 5½ - 7½ barrel

32-20 Winchester "
38-40 "
44-40 "
45 Colt
} $33.00

Any kind of Pistol, Rifle or Shot-gun furnished. Write us for prices

MUST BE SENT BY EXPRESS

HEAVY SADDLE LEATHER

RIFLE HOLSTERS

Plain $6.00
Basket stamp..........$7.00
Flower stamp $10.00
(Give calibre, length, make and model of gun)

No. 25—Hip Pocket Holster

Price—$2.75
Any style made to order. All belts and holsters made of heavy saddle leather.

SKETCHES BY LEE M. RICE (SEE PAGE 126)

We can now offer our customers a series of six true-to-life, pen and ink sketches of life on the range. These pictures are full of life and vivid action, that the man who rides can appreciate and enjoy. One would know, at a glance, that the artist "knew his stuff." True enough, for the artist, Lee M. Rice, is at home on the range and reproduces the free action of the flying hoofs of a cow horse heading off a dodging steer as vividly as that tense moment when a bucker "cuts loose."

Take advantage of this unusual offer of six of these beautiful lithographed reproductions, size 10x14 inches, for only $1.00 (postage prepaid when cash accompanies order).

ELECTRIC CLIPPER

A new "Stewart"—handy, practical, durable — with cord and plug to use in wall socket or any fixture.
Price complete—$15.00

HALTERS

THE JOHNSON IDEAL HALTER

Strong and Durable
Special price per dozen

Heavy oak-tan leather, copper hand rivets.

No. 1—1½ in. extra heavy, double crown, chain throat $3.50
No. 3—1½ in. single crown, no chain $3.00
No. 5—1¼ in. same $2.75

Machine Riveted
No. 7—1¼ in. Horse $2.00
No. 9 — Yearling $1.75
No. 11 — Colt $1.50
No. 15 — Cow $1.50
Lower prices per dozen

JOHNSON ROPE

Braided Cotton
No. 1-X—Extra large $1.10
No. 1 — Regular $1.00
No. 2 — Small Horse 90c
Postpaid

HORSE BLANKETS
Cut No. 1

No. 80—Baker Blanket
Cut No. 3

Cut No. 1
No. 50 — Heavy Burlap, unlined, reinforced at neck and breast, with two sursingles.
68 - $1.75 72 - $1.85 76 - $2.00
No. 52—Heavy Burlap, as above Half lined with good kersey.
68 - $2.25 72 - $2.40 76 - $2.60
No. 54—Heavy Mangled Burlap, lined with heavy kersey, reinforced neck and breast, wide sursingles.
68 - $3.25 72 - $3.50 76 - $3.75
No. 60—Heavy fawn hose duck, lined with heavy fawn kersey, bound neck and breast, 2½-inch heavy sursingles.
68 - $6.00 72 - $6.25 76 - $6.50

BAKER BLANKET—Cut No. 2
No. 80—Genuine 5A Baker Blanket, made of high grade long staple cotton, double twisted yarn, reinforced at neck and breast. Heavy fine-web bias girth sursingles. The superior blanket for more than fifty years, is unequaled for wear and fit.
68-$12.75 72-$13.50 76-$14.25
No. 85—Stable Sheet, made of soft woven hose duck, fawn color reinforced at neck and breast, bound all around in colored webbing, two wide sursingles.
68 - $3.75 72 - $4.00 76 - $4.25
No. 95—Stable Sheet, extra quality old gold soft woven hose duck, reinforced at neck and breast, bound all around with colored webbing, wide sursingles.
Size 68-inch—$4.75 Size 72-inch—$5.25 Size 76-inch—$5.75
No. 060—Long Hoods, made of heavy fawn hose duck, lined throughout with heavy fawn kersey, bound and reinforced edges. Made to button close at neck and breast. Superior for use in open trailers or trucks, or in extreme weather.
Small, Medium and Large—Matches No. 60 Blanket—All sizes $4.75 Each
No. 080—Long Hood, genuine 5A Baker Cloth. Reinforced and bound on edge and at ear and eye holes. Made to button close at neck and breast. Sizes—
Small, Medium and Large. Matches No. 80 Blanket—All sizes $10.50 Each

EYE GOGGLES with ventilated leather sides and heavy isinglass windows. Goggles are attached to the hood by snap fasteners and easily removed when not wanted. Price $3.50 —added to hood prices.

HOBBLES

.No. 5
Medium $1.75
No. 10
Heavy $2.25
No. 15
Ex. Heavy $2.50

No. 20—Figure 8, double leather.....$2.00
No. 22—Figure 8, single leather....... 1.25

PARCEL POST CHART

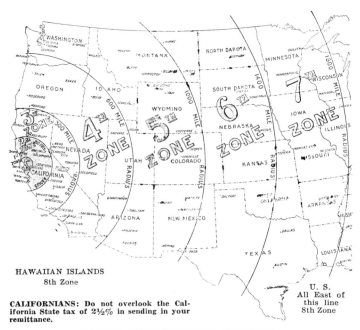

HAWAIIAN ISLANDS
8th Zone

CALIFORNIANS: Do not overlook the California State tax of 2½% in sending in your remittance.

U. S.
All East of this line
8th Zone

Weight in pounds	Local	1st, up to 50 miles	2d, 50 to 150 miles	3d, 150 to 300 miles	4th, 300 to 600 miles	5th, 600 to 1,000 miles	6th, 1,000 to 1,400 miles	7th, 1,400 to 1,800 miles	8th, over 1,800 miles
1	$0.07	$0.08	$0.08	$0.09	$0.10	$0.11	$0.12	$0.14	$0.15
2	.08	.10	.10	.11	.14	.17	.19	.23	.26
3	.08	.11	.11	.13	.17	.22	.26	.32	.37
4	.09	.12	.12	.15	.21	.27	.33	.41	.48
5	.09	.13	.13	.17	.24	.33	.40	.50	.59
6	.10	.14	.14	.19	.28	.38	.47	.59	.70
7	.10	.15	.15	.21	.31	.43	.54	.68	.81
8	.11	.16	.16	.23	.35	.49	.61	.77	.92
9	.11	.17	.17	.25	.38	.54	.68	.86	1.03
*10	.12	.18	.18	.27	.42	.59	.75	.95	1.14
11	.12	.19	.19	.29	.45	.64	.82	1.04	1.25
12	.13	.21	.21	.31	.49	.70	.89	1.13	1.36
13	.13	.22	.22	.33	.52	.75	.96	1.22	1.47
14	.14	.23	.23	.35	.56	.80	1.03	1.31	1.58
15	.14	.24	.24	.37	.59	.86	1.10	1.40	1.69
16	.15	.25	.25	.39	.63	.91	1.17	1.49	1.80
17	.15	.26	.26	.41	.66	.96	1.24	1.58	1.91
18	.16	.27	.27	.43	.70	1.02	1.31	1.67	2.02
19	.16	.28	.28	.45	.73	1.07	1.38	1.76	2.13
20	.17	.29	.29	.47	.77	1.12	1.45	1.85	2.24
21	.17	.30	.30	.49	.80	1.17	1.52	1.94	2.35
22	.18	.32	.32	.51	.84	1.23	1.59	2.03	2.46
23	.18	.33	.33	.53	.87	1.28	1.66	2.12	2.57
24	.19	.34	.34	.55	.91	1.33	1.73	2.21	2.68
25	.19	.35	.35	.57	.94	1.39	1.80	2.30	2.79
26	.20	.36	.36	.59	.98	1.44	1.87	2.39	2.90
27	.20	.37	.37	.61	1.01	1.49	1.94	2.48	3.01
28	.21	.38	.38	.63	1.05	1.55	2.01	2.57	3.12
29	.21	.39	.39	.65	1.08	1.60	2.08	2.66	3.23
30	.22	40	.40	.67	1.12	1.65	2.15	2.75	3.34
31	.22	41	.41	.69	1.15	1.70	2.22	2.84	3.45
32	.23	.43	.43	.71	1.19	1.76	2.29	2.93	3.56
33	.23	.44	.44	.73	1.22	1.81	2.36	3.02	3.67
34	$0.24	$0.45	$0.45	$0.75	$1.26	$1.86	$2.43	$3.11	$3.78
35	.24	46	.46	.77	1.29	1.92	2.50	3.20	3.89
36	.25	47	.47	.79	1.33	1.97	2.57	3.29	4.00
37	.25	48	.48	.81	1.36	2.02	2.64	3.38	4.11
38	.26	49	.49	.83	1.40	2.08	2.71	3.47	4.22
39	.26	.50	.50	.85	1.43	2.13	2.78	3.56	4.33
40	.27	.51	.51	.87	1.47	2.18	2.85	3.65	4.44
41	.27	.52	.52	.89	1.50	2.23	2.92	3.74	4.55
42	.28	.54	.54	.91	1.54	2.29	2.99	3.83	4.66
43	.28	.55	.55	.93	1.57	2.34	3.06	3.92	4.77
44	.29	.56	.56	.95	1.61	2.39	3.13	4.01	4.88
45	.29	.57	.57	97	1.64	2.45	3.20	4.10	4.99
46	.30	.58	.58	.99	1.68	2.50	3.27	4.19	5.10
47	.30	.59	.59	1.01	1.71	2.55	3.34	4.28	5.21
48	.31	.60	.60	1.03	1.75	2.61	3.41	4.37	5.32
49	.31	.61	.61	1.05	1.78	2.66	3.48	4.46	5.43
50	.32	.62	.62	1.07	1.82	2.71	3.55	4.55	5.54
51	.32	.63	.63	1.09	1.85	2.76	3.62	4.64	5.65
52	.33	.65	.65	1.11	1.89	2.82	3.69	4.73	5.76
53	.33	.66	.66	1.13	1.92	2.87	3.76	4.82	5.87
54	.34	.67	.67	1.15	1.96	2.92	3.83	4.91	5.98
55	.34	.68	.68	1.17	1.99	2.98	3.90	5.00	6.09
56	.35	.69	.69	1.19	2.03	3.03	3.97	5.09	6.20
57	.35	70	.70	1.21	2.06	3.08	4.04	5.18	6.31
58	.36	71	.71	1.23	2.10	3.14	4.11	5.27	6.42
59	.36	.72	.72	1.25	2.13	3.19	4.18	5.36	6.53
60	.37	.73	.73	1.27	2.17	3.24	4.25	5.45	6.64
61	.37	.74	.74	1.29	2.20	3.29	4.32	5.54	6.75
62	.38	.76	.76	1.31	2.24	3.35	4.39	5.63	6.86
63	.38	.77	.77	1.33	2.27	3.40	4.46	5.72	6.97
64	.39	.78	.78	1.35	2.31	3.45	4.53	5.81	7.08
65	.39	79	.79	1.37	2.34	3.51	4.60	5.90	7.19
66	.40	.80	.80	1.39	2.38	3.56	4.67	5.99	7.30
67	.40	.81	.81	1.41	2.41	3.61	4.74	6.08	7.41
68	.41	.82	.82	1.43	2.45	3.67	4.81	6.17	7.52
69	.41	.83	.83	1.45	2.48	3.72	4.88	6.26	7.63
70	.42	.84	.84	1.47	2.52	3.77	4.95	6.35	7.74

PARCEL POST SHIPPING WEIGHTS

Every package under 1 lb. charged as 1 lb.; over 1 lb. charged as 2 lbs. and so on. The following table gives average weights which may vary somewhat, but are sufficiently close to enable you to get at the approximate cost of transportation on any article. These weights are for goods packed.

	lbs.		lbs.		lbs.
Axes	3	Holsters	2	Boys	35
Belts	1	Hobbles	2	Stride	35
Boots	6	Kyax	7 to 12	Saddle pockets	6
Bits	2	Martingales	3	Shipping bags	7
Bucking Rolls	2	Overalls	3	Scabbards	4
Blankets	5	Plyers	3	Spurs	3
Cinches	2	Puttees	3	Spur straps	1
Conchas	1	Revolvers	3 to 5	Sursingles	8
Chaps, fur	10	Rifles	8 to 12	Stirrups	4
Chaps, leather	10	Reins	2	Stirrups	4
Cuffs	2	Ropes	4	Taps—long	10
Hats	3	Saddles—		Taps—short	7
Headstalls	2	With taps	45-50	Tarps	12 to 15
Hackamores	2	No taps	40-45	Tents	25 to 50
		Pack	30	Vests	2

Insurance on packages valued to $5.00, 5c; $5.01 to $25.00, 10c; $25.01 to $50.00, 15c; $50.01 to $100.00, 25c; $100.01 to $150.00, 30c; $150.01 to $200.00, 35c. If more than sufficient postage is sent, we will refund the amount in stamps. Insurance fee is in addition to the regular parcel post rates.

Limit of insurance or C.O.D. is $200.00 on a single shipment. When value exceeds this amount we divide into two shipments if possible to keep within the limit. Note the low rate at which saddles can be sent to any post office, thus reaching hundreds of points that formerly required long stage or team hauls from express offices.

SPECIAL REQUEST

Every few days one of our customers sends in an order accompanied by a cut torn out of our catalog.

This cut and those on the reverse side are absolutely lost so far as any future use or reference is concerned, and later on, when someone is looking in the catalog for information regarding these articles, the catalog is useless as far as these articles are concerned.

It is absolutely unnecessary to send us these torn out cuts, the numbers of the articles being all that is necessary, and there is no possibility of mistake if the numbers are sent correctly.

For your own benefit as well as ours, we ask you kindly: DO NOT CUT OUT THE ENGRAVINGS FROM THE CATALOG. SEND THE NUMBER *ONLY* OF THE ARTICLE WANTED.

D.E. WALKER SADDLES

JOHN E. OLSEN
of the Nugget Ranch, with his beautiful three-quarter thoroughbred
Palomino stallion "Golden Laddie Boy"

BEST

IN

THE

WEST

SINCE

1
8
7
0

Mr. Olsen has used a complete Visalia outfit for many years
and declares there are none better.

–: No. 31 :–
MAKE GOOD

VISALIA STOCK SADDLE CO., 2123 MARKET ST.—SAN FRANCISCO, CALIF.

Original catalog (1938) back cover.